TWO VOLTAIREAN PLAYS

Borgo Press Books by FRANK J. MORLOCK

The Chevalier d'Éon and Other Short Farces from the Eighteenth- and Nineteenth-Century French Theatre (Editor)
Chuzzlewit
Congreve's Comedy of Manners
Crime and Punishment
Falstaff (with William Shakespeare, John Dennis, and William Kendrick)
Fathers and Sons
The Idiot
Jurgen
Justine
Lord Jim
Notes from the Underground
Oblomov
Outrageous Women: Lady Macbeth and Other French Plays (editor and translator)
Peter and Alexis
The Princess Casamassima
A Raw Youth
The Stendhal Hamlet Scenarios and Other Shakespearean Shorts from the French (editor and translator)
Two Voltairean Plays: The Triumvirate and Comedy at Ferney (editor)
The Widow's Husband; and, Porthos in Search of an Outfit: Two Dumasian Comedies (editor and translator)

TWO VOLTAIREAN PLAYS

THE TRIUMVIRATE AND COMEDY AT FERNEY

FRANK J. MORLOCK, EDITOR

THE BORGO PRESS
MMXIII

TWO VOLTAIREAN PLAYS

Copyright © 1991, 2004, 2006, 2013 by Frank J. Morlock

FIRST EDITION

Published by Wildside Press LLC

www.wildsidebooks.com

DEDICATION

To my dear friend, Michael Lidsky

CONTENTS

THE TRIUMVIRATE; OR, AFTER CAESAR'S DEATH: A PLAY IN FIVE ACTS, by Voltaire 9
CAST OF CHARACTERS 10
ACT I 11
ACT II 38
ACT III 57
ACT IV 83
ACT V 105
COMEDY AT FERNEY, by Louis Lurine and Albéric Second 127
CAST OF CHARACTERS 128
COMEDY AT FERNEY 129
ABOUT THE EDITOR 203

THE TRIUMVIRATE; OR, AFTER CAESAR'S DEATH: A PLAY IN FIVE ACTS
BY VOLTAIRE

Translated and Adapted by Frank J. Morlock

CAST OF CHARACTERS

OCTAVIAN

MARK ANTHONY

SEXTUS POMPEY

JULIA, daughter of Lucius Caesar

FULVIA, wife of Mark Anthony

ALBINA, Fulvia's servant

AUFIDIUS, Military Tribune

Tribunes, Centurions, Lictors, Soldiers

ACT I

The action takes place on an island in the River Reno, near modern Bologna.

The Triumvirs are carrying out proscriptions and dividing the world. It is dark. Lightning flashes and the sound of thunder. There are rocks, precipices and tents in the distance.

FULVIA

What a frightful night. How celestial wrath

Explodes with justice over this funereal isle.

ALBINA

These sudden quakes, these overturned rocks,

These infernal volcanoes hurling to the heaven,

This river erected, rolling its waves over us,

Have made humans fear the end of the world.

Thunder has devoured this detestable bronze,

These tables of vengeance where fatal engravings,

Shock our eyes with a list of crimes,

With the order for carnage and the names of victims—

You see, indeed, that our proscriptions

Are the horror of heaven as well as Nature.

FULVIA

Let this wild thunder fall on our tyrants,

Which, vainly striking an abhorred earth,

Has destroyed in the hands of our cruel master

The instruments of crime and not the criminals!

I would have seen this isle annihilated,

With the unworthy affronts with which they load Fulvia.

What are our three tyrants doing in this horrid disorder?

What remorse, at least, have they drawn to themselves?

ALBINA

In this island trembling at lightning bursts

Calmly in their tent as they are sharing the world

Of Senate and people they rule the fate

And into bloody Rome they are sending death.

FULVIA

Anthony is giving it to me, o day of ignominy,

He's leaving me, kicking me out, marrying Octavia.

In an odious divorce, I await the infamous writing

I am repudiated; it's me they are proscribing.

ALBINA

He braves you to this degree?

He's doing you this injury?

FULVIA

Is the murderer of Romans perjuring himself?

I have served him too well—

All barbarians are ingrates

He pretends toward me the consideration of state

But this great consideration is only that of a traitor

That clever Octavian is deceiving him with, perhaps.

ALBINA

Octavian loves you—is it probable that today

Your misfortunes are coming from him?

FULVIA

Who can know Octavian? And how different his character

In every respect from the great heart of his father.

I've seen, in the error of his distraction

Pass even Anthony in his passionate outbursts.

I have seen pleasures in search of mad intoxication

I have seen Catos pretend wisdom

After having offered me a criminal love

This Proteus has escaped my chain without return.

Sometimes willful, sometimes bloodthirsty,

Adoring Julia, he proscribes her father;

He hates, he fears Anthony, and is giving him his sister.

Anthony is wild, but Octavian is deceitful.

These are the heroes who rule the earth,

Playing with peace and war,

From whose voluptuous breasts that enchain us

To what masters, great god, do you deliver the universe?

Albina, lions emerging from carnage, Roaring, follow their savage mates.

Tigers make love with ferocity:

Such are the Triumvirs. Embloodied Anthony,

Prepares the detestable marriage feast.

Octavia, has of Julia undertaken the conquest;

And on their day of blood, of sadness, of horror

Love on all sides is mixed with furor:

Julia abhors Octavian, she is only

Concerned with giving her heart to the son of great Pompey.

If Pompey is written in the fatal book

Octavian, by sacrificing him, strikes in him his rival.

These are the springs of destiny, of empire.

These great secrets of state that ignorance admires

From afar they astonish vulgar wits

Close up, they inspire horror and scorn.

ALBINA

What baseness, O heaven, and what tyranny!

What! The masters of the world are ignoramuses!

I pity you. I thought that today Lepidus

Would support you against those two impostors,

Unite Anthony and yourself with Lepidus.

FULVIA

He hardly counts in their homicidal gang.

Scorned pontiff, subaltern tyrant

They have much abused his weak genius,

Odious instrument of their vile caprices

This vile scoundrel submits to his accomplices.

He signs their orders without being consulted

And still thinks he's acting with authority.

But if some delights still remain to me in my troubles,

It's that my tyrants secretly detest each other.

This marriage with Octavia, and her weak attractions

Will prolong the breach—not prevent it.

They know each other too well, they do each other justice

One day I will see them prepare their sacrifice.

Light Discord with the greatest fury

So that their false friendship exposes here its horror.

(Aufidius enters)

FULVIA

Aufidius, what's going on? What is my fate?

To what abasement am I finally condemned?

AUFIDIUS

The divorce is signed with that self-same hand

That poured out long waves of Roman blood.

And soon your tyrants will come to this tent

To share the bloody pillage of the proscribed.

FULVIA

Can I count on you?

AUFIDIUS

Born in your house

If I am serving under Antonius and in his legion

I am still yours alone. In the past my sword

Served Great Pompey in the fields of Thessaly

I blush to be here the slave of passions

Of the conquerors of Pompey and your oppressors—

But what is your decision?

FULVIA

To avenge myself.

AUFIDIUS

No question,

You must, Fulvia.

FULVIA

No matter what it costs me

There is nothing that I fear and in our factions

They count Fulvia in the rank of the greatest number

In my disgrace, Aufidius, I have only one resource:

The party of Pompey is the one I embrace.

And Lucius Caesar has secret friends

Who will know how to join my cause to his interests.

He is, you know, Julia's father;

He's been proscribed; all reconciles me to him.

Is Julia in Rome?

AUFIDIUS

No one is able to find her there.

The rumor ran

All powerful Octavian would have carried her off.

FULVIA

Rape and murder

These are his exploits! These are our laws, Aufidius.

But Pompey's son—is he safe?

What have you learned about it?

AUFIDIUS

His arrest is projected.

And infamous avarice to power subjected

Must cut off such a fine life at the price of gold

Such are the vile Romans.

FULVIA

What! All hope is fleeing from me!

No, I still defy the fate that pursues me;

The tumults of army camps have been my asylum.

My genius was born for our civil wars,

For this terrible century into which I was born.

I intend—but I notice in this bloody abode

The lictors of tyrants—their cowardly satellites

Who occupy the limits of their barbarous camp.

You, whose funereal job keeps you here near them,

Stay—listen to their dark conspiracies

You will warn me and will come to inform me what I must suffer and what must be attempted.

(she leaves with Albina)

AUFIDIUS

Me, Anthony's soldier! To what am I reduced!

For thirty years of labor what execrable fruit.

(As he speaks, the tent of Octavian where Octavian and Anthony are going to speak is brought forward. The lictors surround it, making a half circle. Aufidius places himself at the side of the tent. Octavian and Anthony stand in the tent with a table between them)

ANTHONY

Octavian, it's done, and I repudiate her—

I retie our bonds by marrying Octavia;

But, it's not enough to extinguish those fires,

That jealous interest ignites between the two of us.

Two leaders, always united, are a rare example.

To counsel them they have to be separated.

Twenty times your Agrippa, your confidants, mine,

For as long as we have reigned, have broken our bonds

One companion the more, or at least who will grow to be one

Affecting to appear on the throne with us—

Lepidus, is a phantom, easy to remove, who himself returns to his obscurity.

Let him remain pontiff and preside at festivals

That trembling Rome dedicates to our conquests:

The earth is ours alone, and our legions—

The time has come to fix the fate of nations

Let's especially regulate one—and when all second us

Let's stop squabbling over sharing the world.

(They sit at the table where they are to sign)

OCTAVIAN

For a long while my plans have foreseen your wishes

I wanted the empire to belong to the two of us

Think that I intend Gaul, Illyria,

Spain, Africa, and especially Italy

The Orient is yours—

ANTHONY

Such is my will.

Such is the fate of the world arrested between us.

I am not hiding from myself what your advantage is.

Rome is going to serve you. You will have under your rule

The conquerors of the earth; I will have only kings

I willingly give it up to you. I demand in exchange that your authority, seconding my power

Exterminate forever the remaining outcasts

Of the party of Pompey, and of the traitor Brutus;

Let none of them escape the laws we have set up.

OCTAVIAN

Perhaps they are cemented with enough blood.

ANTHONY

What! You hesitate. I no longer know you.

What can thus trouble your irresolute desire?

OCTAVIAN

Heaven itself has destroyed these cruel lists

ANTHONY

Heavenseconds us by permitting new ones.

Are you afraid of an omen?

OCTAVIAN

And aren't you fearful

Of revolting the earth because of murders?

We want to chain up Roman liberty

We want to govern, not excite more hate.

ANTHONY

Do you call justice inhumanity?

Octavian, a Triumvir adopted by Caesar

If I avenge a friend, do you fear to avenge a father?

You would forget his blood to flatter the vulgar.

To whom would you pretend to grant a pardon

When you had me sacrifice Cicero?

OCTAVIAN

Rome wept at his death.

ANTHONY

It wept in silence.

Cassius and Brutus, reduced to impotence

Might perhaps inspire other nations

With an eternal horror of our proscription.

It lets them depict terrible images

And against our two names revolt the ages.

Assassins of their master and their benefactor,

It's their unworthy names that ought to be in horror.

These are the ingrate hearts it's time to punish.

They alone are criminals, and we are doing justice.

Those who served them, who approved them

Will have some punishment reserved to them.

Twenty thousand warriors perished in our battles

Their funerals are seen with a dry, calm eye

On their extended bodies, victims of death

We fly, without paling, to new battles

And through the treason of a hundred wretched accomplices

We will make too many costly sacrifices to Caesar.

OCTAVIAN

In Rome, on this very day they are still avenging his death.

But know what costs my heart an effort:

Too much horror in the end can stain his vengeance.

I would be more his son if I had his clemency.

ANTHONY

Clemency today can ruin us both.

OCTAVIAN

An excess of cruelty will be more dangerous.

ANTHONY

Do you distrust the people?

OCTAVIAN

They have to be managed

They must be made to love the bridle of slavery

With an indifferent eye they observe the death of the great

But when they fear for themselves, bad luck to tyrants.

ANTHONY

I hear, at my peril, you seek to please them.

You want to become a popular tyrant.

OCTAVIAN

You are always imparting to me some secret plans.

To sacrifice Pompey—will that please Romans?

Today my orders overthrow their idol.

While I am talking to you, they beat him, they strike him

What more do you want?

ANTHONY

You are not abusing me.

It costs you little to order his death.

To our true interests his death would be necessary.

But you wish to be rid of a secret rival

He adored Julia and you were jealous

Your outraged love leads all your blows

Fulfill the agreement of all our undertakings.

OCTAVIAN

Stop.

ANTHONY

Is the guilty man sacred to us?

I want him dead.

OCTAVIAN (rising)

Him? The father of Julia?

ANTHONY

Yes, himself.

OCTAVIAN

Listen—our interest links us.

Marriage binds the knot; but if you persist

In demanding blood to persecute

From this day I am breaking all alliances between us.

ANTHONY

Octavian, I'm too well aware that our intelligence

Will produce discord and deceive our wishes

Let's not rush to such dangerous times.

Do you intend to offend me?

OCTAVIAN

No—but I am a master

Who would spare a proscribed who should not be

proscribed.

ANTHONY

But you yourself, with me, condemned him.

Of all our enemies, he's the most obstinate.

What difference if his daughter was for a moment dear to you?

To our security I owe the father's blood

The inconstant pleasures of a fleeting love

To our great interests are nothing except foreign

Until now, you've shown little tenderness

And I wasn't expecting this excess of weakness.

OCTAVIAN

Of weakness! It's you who dare to blame me?

Today it's Anthony who forbids me to love?

ANTHONY

Both of us have mixed festivities

And pleasures with the fury of arms.

Caesar did it, too. But through sensuality

The course of his exploits was not hindered.

I saw him in Egypt, amorous and cruel

Adoring Cleopatra, and sacrificing her brother.

OCTAVIAN

That was to serve her, I can see you one day,

More blind than he, weaker in your turn.

I know you well enough, whatever may happen

I've scratched out Lucius, and I insist that he live.

ANTHONY

I will consent to it when seeing you sign

The executions of those proscribed not to be spared.

OCTAVIAN

I've already said, I'm weary of carnage

To which Caesar's death forced my courage.

But since of necessity nothing be done by half

That the safety of Rome be affirmed,

I must consummate the horror that brings us together.

(he sits and signs)

Go, Tribune, bear these unhappy edicts.

(to Anthony who sits and signs)

And as for us, may we be forever joined!

ANTHONY

Yes. Aufidius, tomorrow you will escort Fulvia

Her retreat is limited to the country of Apulia

Let me no longer hear her seditious screams.

OCTAVIAN

Let's hear this Tribune who's returning to these parts.

He's coming from Rome and can inform us

With what respect the Senate has completed our laws.

ANTHONY (to Tribune)

Have they accomplished the Triumvirs' plans?

Does blood assure the repose of humanity?

TRIBUNE

Rome trembles and holds its peace amidst executions

What remains for us is to strike some secret conspirators

Some vile enemies of Anthony's and Caesar's,

Remain from the conspirators of the Ides of March,

Who in their last raids conceal their obscure hate

Are going in secret to the people to excite murmurs.

Paulus, Albin, Cotter, the greatest have fallen;

From the proscription few have escaped.

OCTAVIAN

Have they affirmed the conquest of the universe?

And brought the head of the son of Pompey?

For the good of the state, I had to demand it.

TRIBUNE

The gods didn't wish, lords, to grant it to you.

This bold youth, very dear to the Romans,

Appears to their eyes with the virtues of his father,

And when through my efforts, the heads of the proscribed

To the walls of the capitol the rewards are affixed,

Pompey to their safety set forth rewards,

He had by his benefits combated your vengeance.

But when your legions, marching on our heels,

Then, fleeing from Rome, and seeking battle

He advanced to Ceseria, and near the Pyrenees

Joined his destiny to that of Cato's son.

While in the Orient, Cassius and Brutus

Conspirators very famous for their false virtues

To their weak party gave a bit of audacity,

They dared to defy you in the fields of Thrace.

ANTHONY

Pompey has escaped!

OCTAVIAN

Don't be alarmed!

No matter what place he may be in, death is on his heels;

If my father owed his triumph in Pharsalia

I expect against the son an equal fortune

And the name of Caesar by which I am honored

Has made his ruin a sacred duty to my arm.

ANTHONY

Let's prepare this great enterprise suddenly

But let our interests never divide us.

The blood of great Caesar is already joined to mine

Your sister is my wife; and this double bond

Must affirm the yoke by which our victorious hands

Will hold trembling nations at our knees.

(Anthony and his party leave)

OCTAVIAN (alone—the Tribune at a distance)

What will all these knots do? We are two tyrants!

Powers of the earth—do you have relatives?

Julia was born in the blood of Caesars—

And far from seeking my useful alliance

She looks on this sad union

Only as one of the decrees of proscription.

(To Tribune)

Come back!— What, Pompey has escaped my vengeance?

What—Julia is in communication with him?

Is she unaware in what parts she has come?

TRIBUNE

Her father is aware, and doesn't doubt

Himself to prepare the flight of his daughter.

OCTAVIAN

What is my overly seduced reason being informed of?

What! When it's necessary to govern the consternated universe

Surrounded by enemies, environed by murder

Stained by the blood of the proscribed I sacrifice to my father

Detested by Romans, perhaps, by a brother-in-law,

In the midst of war, in the breast of factions

To other passions my heart is open.

What unheard of mixture, what astonishing intoxication

With love, ambition, crimes, weakness!

What devouring cares are coming to consume me!

Destroyer of humans, is it suitable for you to love?

CURTAIN

ACT II

AUFIDIUS

Yes, I heard everything, the blood and the carnage

Cost nothing, madame, to your flighty spouse

I am always astonished at the lawless heart

Plunged into licentiousness, abandoned to vice

In the frightful pleasures which divide his life.

It maintains a calm and reflective cruelty

Even Octavian, Octavian seems unworthy of it;

He regretted the blood in which his arm is bathed

He was no longer himself, he seemed to blush

For having had Anthony as his accomplice for so long.

Perhaps he feigns repentance in the eyes of his partisans

Or perhaps his soul, secretly revolted,

Was shocked by its own fury.

I'm unaware, if one day he was born to experience

Some feeble return to human justice.

But he struggled over the choice of victims

And I've seen him tremble in signing so many crimes.

FULVIA

What is this weak and vain remorse to my affronts?

Each of them in turn gives me death.

Octavian whom you believe less harsh and less ferocious

Hides a more atrocious heart beneath a human air;

He acts barbarously and speaks softly

I see the profound darkness of his mind

The sphinx is his emblem, and it tells us he prefers

That symbol of trickery to his father's eagles.

He sets all his efforts to deceiving the universe.

Incapable of virtues, at least he feels them

And the other one, still in his warrior virtues

Has raging vices in his crude soul.

They dare to banish me; that's the thing I wish

I don't insist on whining before them,

To keep breathing an air they have empoisoned.

Let's fulfill without delay the orders they are giving me.

Let's leave. In what lands, in what unknown places

Shall we not feel abhorred like Rome?

I will find the balm of my hate everywhere.

(Enter Albina)

ALBINA

Madame, hope for everything, Pompey is at Cesena

Thousands of Romans crowd about his path

His name and his misfortune produce soldiers

They say he joins valor to diligence

He's bringing vengeance to this barbaric island

That the three assassins are proscribed in their turn

That he's placed a bounty on their impure blood

They even say that Brutus is advancing toward the Tiber

That the earth is avenged, and that, at last, Rome is Free.

This news has already spread through the entire camp.

And the soldier murmurs or remains distracted.

FULVIA

They talk too much, Albina, a blessing so desirable

Is too prompt and too great to be realistic

But these rumors at least may console me

If my persecutors learn to tremble.

AUFIDIUS

It's the foundation of this popular rumor, a bit of truth causes vulgar mistake

Pompey was able to deceive the sword of the assassins

That's a lot—all the rest is in the lap of destiny.

I know that he was marching toward the walls of Cesena;

Of his departure at least, the news is certain

And the uproar that's spreading confirms to us today

That Roman hearts are turned towards him.

But his danger is great, whole legions

Are marching on his passage, and encircle the frontiers

Pompey is bold, and his rivals, prudent.

FULVIA

Prudence is especially necessary to evil doers,

But often it deceives; a fortunate boldness

Confounds in act the one who deliberates.

In the end, Pompey approaches. United by fury

Our common interests announce an avenger to me.

Revolutions, fatal or prosperous of the sort which lead all are ordinary gamblers

Fortune shows to our eyes, mounted in his chariot

Sulla, the two Mariuses, and Pompey and Caesar

It has precipitated these thunderbolts of war

With their blood, in turn, they've reddened the earth.

Rome has changed laws, tyrants and fetters

Already our Triumvirs are experiencing reversals

Cassius and Brutus threaten Italy

I will go find Pompey in the sands of Libya

After my two affronts, unworthy sufferings

I shall console myself by troubling the universe

Remind Spain and agitated Gaul

That I have been persecuted because of their liberty

Can I, in the blood of others, lucky monster

Expiate the crimes I've committed for them?

Pardon, Cicero, Rome's fortunate genius,

My fate has avenged you; your executions have punished me.

But I will die happy in such great misfortunes

If I die like you, the scourge of tyrants

(to Aufidius)

Before leaving, try to find out

If some ray of hope can light us.

Profit by moments in which the worried soldiers

In the camp of tyrants appear shaken up.

Announce their Pompey—at this great name, perhaps,

They will repent having another master.

Go!

(Julia appears hidden amidst the rocks. Aufidius leaves.)

FULVIA

What do I see in the distance in these deserted rocks.

On the escarped shores of half open abysses

That presents to my eyes the still trembling earth.

ALBINA

See, or I am deceived—a dying woman.

FULVIA

Is there some victim sacrificed hereabouts?

Perhaps the tyrants exposed her before our eyes

And by means of such a spectacle would teach me

What I am to expect from their triumvirate.

Go—I hear her outburst and her screams.

Recall her wits into her oppressed heart.

Lead her to me.

(Albina goes to Julia and brings her to Fulvia, supporting her)

JULIA

Vengeful gods that I adore

Hear me! See for whom I implore you!

Aid a hero—or make me die.

FULVIA

I feel myself softening from her plaintive tones.

JULIA

Where am I? Into what place have the waves cast me?

I run about, trembling, my view dazzled.

Where to go? What hand here is offering me succor?

And who is coming to revive my wretched life?

FULVIA

Her quavering voice is not unknown to me:

Let's come forward. Heavens! Who do I see! Can I believe my eyes!

Fates who play with wretched mortals,

Are you leading Julia into these criminal places?

Am I not mistaken! There's no doubting it, it's she!

JULIA

What! near Anthony, great gods! It's his cruel spouse.

I am lost.

FULVIA

What do you fear from me?

Do unfortunates inspire fear?

Look at me without trembling, I am far from being feared.

You wretched, and I am more to be pitied.

JULIA

You!

FULVIA

What events, and which irritated gods

Have brought Julia into these detestable parts?

JULIA

I don't know where I am. A terrible flood,

Which seemed to engulf a guilty earth

With frightful quaking, devouring lightning

Plunged my followers into overflowing waves

One lone warrior escaped death.

I marched for some time over this rocky isle.

In the distance my eyes saw tents, soldiers,

These rocks hid my terror and my steps

The one who guided me hardly ceased to appear

When I recognized myself before you.

I am dying.

FULVIA

Ah, Julia.

JULIA

Eh, what! You are sighing.

FULVIA

With your ills and mine, my feelings are torn apart.

JULIA

You are suffering like me! What misfortune opposes you?

Alas, where are we?

FULVIA

At a crime scene.

In this execrable island where three monsters unite,

Bloodying the world and remaining unpunished.

JULIA

What! It's here that Anthony and the barbarous Octavian

Condemned Pompey and enslaved the world.

FULVIA

It's under these pavilions that they rule our fate

Right here, even, they signed Pompey's death warrant.

JULIA

Sustain me, great gods!

FULVIA

The tigers have left

This frightful retreat, their bloody troupe

Is marching at this very instant to the opposite shore

The place in which I'm speaking to you is less exposed

My tents are here; don't let anyone see us.

Come; calm this trouble is which your soul is bathed.

JULIA

And the wife of Anthony is my support here?

FULVIA

Thanks to his crimes, I am no longer his wife.

Henceforth, I have no greater role than you do.

Fate, through pity, has joined us to each other.

What's become of Pompey?

JULIA

Ah! What have you told me?

Why seek information about a wretched proscript?

FULVIA

Is he safe? Speak in confidence

I witness here to the gods, to Rome, and to my vengeance

My hate for Octavian and my jealous distractions

That my efforts will answer for Pompey and for you,

That I will defend you at the peril of my life.

JULIA

Alas, so it's really in you that I must trust?

If you, too, have known adversity,

Doubtless you would not have the cruelty

To finish my life, and betray my misery.

You see where the wrath of the gods had led me.

Through bizarre luck you have in your hands

The fate of Pompey, and the blood of Caesars.

I joined these names; the interest of the country

Formed our marriage in the midst of war.

Rome, Pompey, and myself, all are ready to perish.

Do you have virtue enough to dare to help them?

FULVIA

I shall dare yet more. If he's on this shore

Just let him dare to second my courage.

Yes—I believe that heaven, so long merciless

Has led all three of us by the hand to avenge ourselves.

Yes! I will arm his hand against tyranny

Speak and fear nothing.

JULIA

Wandering, pursued,

I fled the assassin's blade with him

Rome inundated the highways with them—

We were going towards his camp—already his renown

Had assembled the refuse of an army at Cesena.

Through dangers reborn near us

He led my uncertain and trembling step.

Death was everywhere; the bloody henchmen

Occupied the limits of the plain of Cesena

Night misdirected us toward this funereal shore,

Where tyrants reign, where death presides.

Our fatal error was not noticed

When thunderbolts struck our lost following—

The earth, roaring, opened beneath our feet

This place, indeed, is one of death.

FULVIA

Well! Is he still in this terrible island?

If he dares show himself, his ruin is certain.

He is dead.

JULIA

I know it.

FULVIA

Where must I seek him?

Has he been able to hide himself in some secret asylum?

JULIA

Ah, Madam.

FULVIA

Get to the end: there's too much suspicion

I pardon your love for a suspicion that offends me.

Speak—I'll do everything.

JULIA

Can I believe it so?

FULVIA

I swear it to you once again.

JULIA

Well—he's here.

FULVIA

That's enough, let's go.

JULIA

He's searching for a passage

To leave this savage island with me.

And, no longer seeing him in these desert rocks

Shadows of death covered my eyes.

I was dying, when heaven, for once favorable

Presented to me through you—a helping hand.

(Enter Tribune)

TRIBUNE

Madame, a stranger is here near you.

The Triuvirs, jealous of their authority

Have forbidden all entry to the island by any mortal.

JULIA

Ah, I witness the fidelity you have sworn to me.

TRIBUNE

I must lead her before their tribunal.

FULVIA

Beware of obeying this fatal order.

JULIA

Well, I thus swallow the honor of my ancestors.

Soldiers of Triumvirs—go tell your masters

That Julia, dragged into this frightful place

Is awaiting to leave, generous help

That everywhere I am free, and that they can know

What respect they owe to the blood from which I am

born

To my rank, to my sex, to hospitality

To the laws of nations, and mankind

Lead me to your home, magnanimous Fulvia.

FULVIA

Your noble pride is not demented

It increases mine; and it's not in vain

That fate leads you to this inhuman shore

Let me not be deceived in my plans.

JULIA

O Gods! Take my life and watch over Pompey!

Gods! If you deliver me to my persecutors

Arm me with courage equal to their fury.

CURTAIN

ACT III

POMPEY

I can no longer find her. What! My fatal destiny

Leads her to my tyrants, delivers her to my rival!

There they are, I see them. These horrible pavilions

Where our murderers, retired and calm

Order carnage with serene eyes,

The way one gives a feast and games to Romans.

O Pompey! O my father! great, unfortunate man!

What then is the destiny of the defenders of Rome?

O Gods! who follow the standards of malefactors.

Why is it that the universe is made for Caesars?

I watched Cato perish: their judge and your image

The Superas died in the desert of Carthage,

Cicero, you are no more, and you your head and your hands

Have served the triumph of the worst of mankind.

My fate is going to join me to these great victims

The sword of Achilles and that of Septimus

Criminal instruments of a vile king of Egypt

Shed the blood of the greatest of mortals.

It's only by his death that his son resembles him.

Brigands united, assembled for pillage

A pretended Caesar, a son of Copias!

Who commands death and flees battles,

In their calm rage decree my death!

Octavian is finally master of the world and of Julia.

Of Julia! Ah, tyrant, this last blow of fate

Alters my mind, struggling against death.

Detestable rival, infamous usurper,

You are assassinating me only to ravish my wife.

And I'm the one who is delivering her to your unworthy passions.

You reign, I die, and I am leaving you happy!

And your flatterers, quaking over a heap of victims

Have already adorned your crimes with the name Augustus!

Who is this assassin who's advancing toward me?

(sword in hand)

Approach, and may Octavian expire with you.

AUFIDIUS

Judge better of a soldier who served your father.

POMPEY

And you are serving a tyrant.

AUFIDIUS

I abjure him, and I hope not to be useless in this frightful place

To the son, to the worthy son of an unfortunate hero.

Lord, I am coming to you on behalf of Fulvia.

POMPEY

Is this a new snare that tyranny extends?

Are you coming to deliver me to her barbarous spouse?

AUFIDIUS

I am coming to snatch you from the greatest peril.

POMPEY

Great Gods, is humanity known here?

AUFIDIUS

Deign to glance, at least, on this letter.

(he gives him notebooks)

POMPEY

Julia! O heaven! Julia! Is it really true?

AUFIDIUS

Read.

POMPEY

O Fortune! O my eyes, are you abused?

Unexpected return of my prosperous destiny,

I moisten these divine characters with tears.

(he reads)

"Fate appears to change, and Fulvia is for us;

Hear this Roman, save my spouse."

Whoever you may be, pardon, to you I confide myself.

I believe you generous on the fidelity of Julia.

What—Fulvia has taken care of her fate and mine!

What can engage her? What interest?

AUFIDIUS

Her own.

Anthony is abandoning her with ignominy.

She is the greatest enemy of these tyrants.

She cannot set limits to her hate, and her plans

To steal your life from the daggers of assassins.

There is no peril her wrath will not brave.

She intends to avenge you.

POMPEY

Yes, we'll avenge ourselves on Octavian

Raised in Asia, in the midst of battles

I knew him only through his assassinations

And in the field of honor, that he perhaps dreads,

His eyes, which he had lowered would not have seen me appear.

At least Anthony has virtue as a soldier.

It's true that my arm has never fought him

And since my father expired to a traitor

We were enemies without ever knowing each other.

Let's begin with Octavian, let's go, and let my hand

At the edge of my tomb, plunge in his breast.

AUFIDIUS

Come then to Fulvia, and be aware that she is prepared

If need be to deliver the head of Octavian to you.

I will test the fidelity of some veterans

Who, like me, served under your illustrious father.

They are changing sides in the civil wars.

To Fulvia's designs they may be useful.

Self-interest, which does all things, might engage them

To give you a retreat and even to avenge you.

POMPEY

I will be able to snatch Julia from this perfidious man?

I can sacrifice this murderer to the Romans?

Octavian will perish?

AUFIDIUS

Lord, don't doubt it.

POMPEY

Let's march.

(Enter Julia)

JULIA

What are you doing? Where are your steps taking you?

They're looking for you, they're pursuing all those that

this storm

Cast like me on this frightful shore.

Your father was delivered to assassins in Egypt

Enemies no less bloody surround.

The friendship of Fulvia is funereal and cruel;

It's one more danger that she trails after her.

They watch her, they spy on her, and everything makes me tremble.

In these horrible parts I'm afraid to speak to you.

Let's regain the rocks and dark caverns

Where night is going to bring its favorable shade.

Tomorrow, at first break of day, fly these tyrants.

We'll leave this fatal place to death

They are going to embloody the Tiber far from your eyes.

Don't rush, tomorrow you are free.

POMPEY

Noble and tender half of an unfortunate warrior

O you! Like Rome, object of all my prayers!

Let me oppose myself to destiny which outrages me.

If I were worthy of my courage in these parts

Into the camp of Brutus, or into that of Cato

You wouldn't see me waiting for Fulvia.

An uncertain help against tyranny.

The Gods have led us into these bloody deserts

Let's march on the only path the gods have opened for me.

JULIA

At this moment, Octavian is at Fulvia's

If you are recognized, your life is done.

AUFIDIUS

Lord, fear rather to be discovered here

This passage is open to tribunes, to soldiers.

Between these dangers what do you intend to do?

JULIA

Pompey, in the name of the Gods, in the name of your father,

Whose bad luck follows you, and who was ruined

Only by too much trust, and too much virtue

Take pity on an alarmed spouse.

Do we have a party? friends, an army?

Three all-powerful masters have destroyed the Romans.

You are alone against a thousand assassins.

They ae coming, it's over with, and I see them appear.

AUFIDIUS

Ah, let yourself be led, they might recognize you.

Time presses, come, you will be ruined for nothing.

JULIA

I shan't leave you.

POMPEY

To what am I reduced!

(Octavian appears in the distance with lictors)

I intend to speak to you; don't flee, Julia.

JULIA

Aufidius, take me to Fulvia's tents.

OCTAVIAN

Stay, I insist you—who is that Roman?

Is he one of your suite?

JULIA

Ah! I am succumbing at last.

AUFIDIUS

He's one of my soldiers whose useful courage

Is distinguished in Rome in these days of carnage.

And from Rome, by my order, he arrives today.

OCTAVIAN (to Pompey)

Speak: what's Pompey doing?

Where has Pompey fled?

POMPEY

He's not fleeing any more, Octavian.

Before day's end you will see him appear.

OCTAVIAN

You know in what condition he must be presented

In a word, it's his head that he must present to me

And you ought to be informed what the reward is.

POMPEY

It's public enough.

JULIA

O terror!

POMPEY

O vengeance!

TRIBUNE (entering)

You are obeyed: thanks to your lucky fate

At this moment, Pompey is captive or dead.

OCTAVIAN

What are you saying?

TRIBUNE

His followers were advancing in the plain

Which extends from Pisaner to the rampart of Cesena

The rebels, soon surrounded and surprised

Had the worthy reward of their cemetery.

POMPEY

Ah, heaven.

TRIBUNE

From the valor they all showed

You'd think they were fighting under the eyes of their master.

POMPEY (aside)

I'm losing all my friends!

TRIBUNE

If he's among the dead

Your soldiers will place the body at your feet.

If he's living, if he flees, no question he'll fall

Into the trap our hands have stretched on his path

He cannot escape the death that awaits him.

OCTAVIAN

Go, continue this important service

You, Aufidius, at all times I test your zeal

I know that Anthony finds a faithful warrior in you

Go: if this soldier can be of use today

Remember, especially, to answer for him.

You, lictors, arrest the first bold one

Who comes, without my order, into this solitary place.

POMPEY (aside)

Come guide my fury.

JULIA

O Gods, who hear me,

Into what new peril are you thrusting us!

OCTAVIAN (stopping Julia)

I already told you, you must listen to me.

Your landing in this island has rightfully surprised me.

But stop being afraid of me, and calm your heart.

JULIA

Lord, I fear nothing, but shiver from horror.

OCTAVIAN

Perhaps you'll change as you know Octavian.

JULIA

I hate the fate of Romans, he treats me as a slave

You might respect my name and my misfortune.

OCTAVIAN

Know that I am the protector of you both.

The respect of Romans and mankind awaits you;

The name you bear, and their prayers demand you;

I must lead you there, and the blood of Caesars

Must not only triumph by entering its ramparts.

Why did you leave them? May I not know

What steals you from Rome, where heaven gave you birth?

JULIA

Ask me rather, why, in these horrible times

Rome still has inhabitants.

Ruin and death is declared on all sides.

My father was proscribed—and that's my reply.

OCTAVIAN

My cares are watching over him.

His life's assured

I've protected him; you make him sacred.

JULIA

So—I must bless your laws and your rule

Because you allow my father to breathe?

OCTAVIAN

He took arms against me—but all that's forgotten.

Don't imitate him in his hostility.

—But in the end what brought you near me?

JULIA

The wrath of the gods determined to injure me.

OCTAVIAN

The Gods will calm down. My strict justice

Has avenged the hero who adopted me. It's suitable for me to honor in Julia

The blood, the august blood from which you descend.

In Rome, I ought to count you as a demi-god

That the world reveres in your ancestors.

JULIA

You!

OCTAVIAN

A son of Caesar must never permit

That they dare place you in foreign hands.

JULIA

You, his son! O hero! O generous victor

What son have you chosen? Who is your successor?

Caesar left you his power to share.

His magnanimity is not your inheritance

If he shed some citizens' blood

It was in battle, spilling his own.

It's by other exploits that you intrigue for power.

He knew how to pardon and you know how to proscribe;

Prodigal of benefactions, and you of assassinations.

You are not his son; I don't know you.

OCTAVIAN

He speaks to me through you, Julia, he pardons you

The injurious names that your mistake gives me.

Don't reproach me for these strict arrests

That tears from my justice an unfortunate duty.

Peace will succeed days of vengeance.

JULIA

What! you will give me a ray of hope!

OCTAVIAN

You can do all.

JULIA

Who? Me?

OCTAVIAN

You ought to suppose

That is the sole way of disarming me.

And that is the cause and pledge of my clemency.

JULIA

You speak of clemency in the midst of carnage?

Alas, so much blood, torture and death

Have been able to let into you some outburst of remorse.

If you at least fear this public hate

This horror attached to tyrannical power

Or if some virtues are germinating in your heart

Don't soil honor by placing a price on them

Don't debase their august character

Is it your passions that will make you more just?

Be great for your self alone.

OCTAVIAN

Go, I hear you

And actually, I foresaw your insulting refusal

A criminal rival, an enemy race—

JULIA

Who?

OCTAVIAN

You demand it! You know very well, Julia

The one who, for a long time has been the object of my wrath.

What about Pompey?

JULIA

Ah, cruel—what name are you saying?

Pompey is far from me; who told you that I love him?

OCTAVIAN

Who told me? Your tears! Who told me? You yourself.

Pompey is far from you and you regret it!

You think to soften me by insulting me

When at last your imprudent flight from Rome

From the breast of your parents drags you in his suite.

JULIA

Thus you add shame to your furies.

Ah! It's not up to you to teach me morals.

I am not reduced to such shame.

And it's not to you that I justify myself.

I left my country that you embloodied

My parents and my gods—that you persecute!

I had a duty to leave Rome where you were going to appear.

My father ordered it, you, perhaps, know it.

It's you I was fleeing; my funereal fate

Placed me in your hands as I was fleeing you.

Command, if you must, the enslaved earth

My heart does not depend on your tyranny

You can do what you will with Rome, but nothing to my duty.

OCTAVIAN

You're as ignorant of my rights as my power.

You're mistaken, Julia, and you may learn

That without me, Lucius cannot choose a son-in-law,

That it's I, especially, who must be obeyed.

Already, Rome awaits me; be prepared to leave.

JULIA

Behold now this great heart, this magnanimous hero

Who wants to deserve the esteem of the pacified world.

Behold this happy reign of peace and gentleness;

He was a murderer! He's become a mere rapist!

OCTAVIAN

He was fair towards you, but—whatever he may be—

Know that scorn won't do for a master.

Whether you love Pompey or another rival

Encouraged by you seeks the fatal honor

Of daring for a single moment to dispute my conquest.

He shall know my vengeance; it will claim his head.

He's a new proscribed that I must condemn.

And I swear to you not to pardon him.

JULIA

As for me, I swear here to Rome and its divine genius

All these heroes armed against tyranny

The pure blood of Caesars, which you are not—

That to your proscriptions you will add my death.

Before you force this independent soul

To join her pure hand to your blood covered one,

The murderers that in Rome committed your furors

Are, I expect, the forerunners.

A new Appius has found Virginia

Her blood will have avenged: it was a homeland

Rome still struggles in. Women at all times

Have been accustomed, in our walls, to punish tyrants.

The kings, you know, were expelled for them.

New Tarquin, tremble!

(she leaves)

OCTAVIAN

What new insults!

What reproaches overwhelm my oppressed heart!

This heart has told me more than she said

A cruel man is hated; I've experienced that.

I am already punished for my total power,

Hardly do I govern, hardly have I tasted

This power that I'm envied for!—which costs me so much.

You intend to reign, Octavian, and you cherish glory.

You want your name to live in memory

It will bear shame to your posterity

To be forever hated! What immortality.

But to be so by Julia—and justly so!

To hear that decree which alone causes you torture

Can you support this doleful torment

When your mind's distracted by contrary wishes?

Where does the harm that it hates, and flees the blessing it loves!

Which searches ways to deceive itself, and which hates itself?

Must love then add to my fury?

Ah! love was made to soften our morals

Unworthy sensuality corrupted my youth

Ambition with its rage succeeded that.

By what new torment am I letting myself be carried away!

How many enemies to vanquish and how to break them?

Manes of Great Caesar! O my master, o my father!

By Brutus sacrificed, but by Brutus revered

Terrible hero, and gentle to all your enemies.

You left me the empire conquered by your valor

Half of this burden overwhelmed my youth

I have only your faults, I have only your weakness

And I feel my heart struggling with remorse

That I do not dare to dispute virtue with you.

CURTAIN

ACT IV

ALBINA

When beneath your pavilions occupied by her fear

Invoking in secret the ghost of Great Pompey

Outbursts in mouth, and death in her eyes

Julia calls in vain on hell and the gods

You are leaving her, Fulvia, to her mortal sorrow.

FULVIA

Let her complain to the gods—I am going to act for her

I'm awaiting Pompey here!

ALBINA

Eh! Couldn't you

Hasten your feet from this island together with them?

FULVIA

No, the attentive furor of our enemies

Covers both shores with murderers.

Nothing can get us out of this gulf of horror.

I'm staying here yet one more day, and it's because of their misfortune.

ALBINA

What can you hope for in a day?

FULVIA

Death; but vengeance, too.

ALBINA

Eh! Can one be avenged on the all-powerful?

FULVIA

Yes, when one fears nothing.

ALBINA

In our vain sorrows

The weapons of an unlucky sex are tears.

The powerful crush beneath their feat the weak who threaten them.

And as they crush them, laugh at their feeble audacity.

FULVIA

They won't be insulting Fulvia anymore.

They won't play with my superfluous tears.

I know that these pirates, famished for plunder

In completing my disgrace have sworn my ruin.

They will steal from me the wealth my father left me

They'll give it as a dowry to my proud rival.

But trust me, Albina, the nuptial pomp

Can yet be changed into real mourning.

And every usurper is near his shroud.

I've taken the only decision that remains to my lot

Pompey's quarrel and mine is mutual.

I await him—that suffices.

ALBINA

He is alone—without help.

FULVIA

He will have help from me.

ALBINA

You're risking his life.

FULVIA

I am lavishing mine. Go—return to Julia

Support her despair and her weak strength

Bring her your advice, her age needs it.

And leave to me the complete care of my frightful fate.

ALBINA

The state I see you in shocks and affects me.

FULVIA

Take your fear elsewhere, go—leave me alone, I tell you.

Pompey will soon be here. I see him. Vengeful god,

Let our affronts unite our fury

(Exit Albina)

(to Pompey)

Are you decided?

POMPEY

I've consulted my glory

I feared that it won't see too black a deed

In the unheard of murder we're busy with.

FULVIA

It speaks with Rome; it tells you: strike!

They are leaving tomorrow, these destroyers of the world.

They are leaving triumphant, and this profound night

Is the time, the only time, when we two,

Without other help than ourselves, can avenge Rome on them.

Would you be hesitating?

POMPEY

No: my hands will be ready

I want to fight the three heads of this Hydra

I can sacrifice only one of my enemies

Octavian is the greatest—he's the one I choose.

FULVIA

You are risking death.

POMPEY

That ennobles my cause

It's a small thing for me to dispose of this unworthy blood.

Vengeance is a small thing; I would only blush

To strike without peril, and without knowing how to die.

FULVIA

You are doing yet more, you are avenging the nation

And the innocent blood that rises and screams

You are serving the universe.

POMPEY

I've decided.

The assassin of Rome must be assassinated.

Thus died Caesar—he was brave and clement.

And we should pardon this cowardly Octavian!

What Brutus could do, I cannot!

And I would borrow other arms for my Caesar!

The die is cast. Let Aufidius come.

FULVIA

He's watching—near us—in this homicidal camp.

Let him be called. The campfires are almost out

And silence reigns in these inhuman regions.

(Aufidius enters)

AUFIDIUS

Sleep spreads its favorable poppies there

When the walls of Rome, delivered to carnage

Echo with desperate screams

That mothers and daughters cast toward heaven

Over the stretched out bodies of sons and fathers.

Blood streams in Rome; Octavian sleeps in peace.

POMPEY

Vengeance, awaken! Death, punish his crimes!

Tell me in what place his tents are erected?

FULVIA

You've noticed these heaped up rocks

Which leave a passage to their secret valleys

Irrigated by a stream bordered by cypresses.

Anthony's pavilion is near the shore,

Pass, and disdain to avenge my outrage;

Not far distant you will find the enclosure

Where the barbarous son of clement Caesar is.

Advance, avenge yourself.

AUFIDIUS

A bloody troop

At all hours of the night surrounds his tent.

Frightful imitators of their leader's pleasures

They sleep nearby in the breast of honor.

POMPEY

You have prepared your faithful slave?

FULVIA

He's waiting for you: go straight to Octavian's bed.

POMPEY

I am leaving in your hands, in this cruel retreat,

The object, the only object that I love in life.

The only one who can unite two fatal families

Two races of heroes—in misfortune equal.

The blood of true Caesars; be careful of her fate.

Instruct her heart to bear my death.

Let her invisage less my ruin than my glory.

That dying to avenge her, I live in memory.

That's all that I wish.—But, in bearing my blows.

I am leaving you exposed, and I shiver for you.

Anthony is master of your life hereabouts

He can avenge on you, Octavia's brother.

FULVIA

Who? Him! Who—this mortal without modesty or fidelity?

This oppressor of Rome, of the world, of me?

He—who dares to exile me? What! In my enterprise

You think that one tyrant, that one death will suffice me?

Did you imagine that I don't know,

Like you, how to bring and suffer death?

That I would be impotently devoured by my sorrows?

See the bloody dwellings of the tyrants

It's a school of murder, and I've needs be been formed by it.

They're animated with their raging mind set.

Their law must become mine, I have to follow it.

Anthony must die, and not that I live.

He will perish I tell you.

POMPEY

And by whom?

FULVIA

By my hand.

POMPEY

Dare you actually carry out such a bold plan?

FULVIA

Dare you doubt it? Destiny joins us

To free the earth and to die together.

Let the Triumvirate be abolished by the two of us,

In the tomb both of us dwell enshrouded

I have lived too much like them; the whole of my life

Has conformed to horrors with which the gods have filled it.

And Pompey, descending to Hell without fright

Is going to drag Octavian down there with me and Anthony.

AUFIDIUS

No, hope still, the soldiers of these traitors

Have sometimes changed flags and masters

They betrayed Lepidus! Today, they might

Give mercenary support to the son of Pompey.

To win over Romans, to force their homage

All that's necessary is a great name, courage, and gold.

They saw Marcus cling at his heals

The same assassins paid to kill him.

We will seduce some, we will fight the rest.

This desperate blow may be funereal for you—

But it can succeed. Brutus and Cassius,

Had not, after all, better conceived plans.

Bold avengers of the common cause

They struck down Caesar and tempted Fortune

They should have died a thousand times in the Senate

They still live; they share the state

In Rome, perhaps, I'll see them with you

My warriors are instantly going to appear at your heels

We will follow you closely—the time's come. Let's march.

POMPEY

I invoke you, Brutus! I am imitating you. Strike!

(Pompey leaves with Aufidius)

JULIA

He's escaping me, he's fleeing me—o heaven, has he deceived me?

Alas! Fatal altar! Manes of Great Pompey!

Has your son prostrated himself to me before you

To betray my sorrows and abandon me?

FULVIA

If misfortune comes to him, arm yourself with courage.

JULIA

What horrible language!

If misfortune comes to him!

Has it?

FULVIA

No, but have a stronger heart, more elevated.

JULIA

It is; but it shivers, you hate and I love

I was everything for Pompey and not for myself.

—What's he doing?

FULVIA

He's serving you. The torches around here

With their weak lights no longer reach my eyes.

Sleep! Sleep of death, favor my rage!

JULIA

Where are you hurrying to?

FULVIA

Stay; I have pity on your age

With your sad love affair and so many sorrows

Shiver if need be; leave me to my fury.

(Exit Fulvia)

JULIA

What's she trying to tell me; and what's being prepared?

Retreat of murderers—frightful and barbarous island

I had actually foreseen that you will be my tomb.

Albina, can you instruct me on my new misfortune?

Is Pompey discovered? Is he seeing his last hour?

Is there no hope? Is it time for me to die?

I am ready, speak!

ALBINA

In this horrible night

I am unaware, like you, if he's succumbed or has fled;

If Fulvia will be able to support death

She's following the advice of blind rage

Let her sudden distractions not captivate her,

She's exposing Pompey instead of serving him.

JULIA

I expected that; and when my fate

In this frightful storm led me near her

I didn't flatter myself that I'd reached a safe haven

I know that here is the reteat of Death.

I am lost, Albina, and not deceived.

The daughter of a Caesar, the widow of a Pompey

Will be worthy, at least, in these extremities

Of the blood she's received, of the name that she bears.

They won't see me dishonor his ashes.

No useless screams that they disdain to hear

Shall blush to survive him and deceive my sorrows.

With uncertain hopes of finding avengers.

To affront death, he escapes my sight

He feared my weakness; he knew me ill.

If he expects me to live, he outrages me indeed.

Let's go.

(Pompey enters)

O Gods! Pompey!

POMPEY

He's dead, it's over with.

JULIA

Who?

POMPEY

The universe is free.

JULIA

O Rome! O my country!

Octavian is dead through you?

POMPEY

Yes, I served you.

I've punished the oppressor of you—and the earth.

JULIA

O unheard of success! Very lucky day!

POMPEY

His guards, drowsy in their infamous intoxication

Allowed free access to my avenging hand

One of his favorites, one of his assassins

An odious minister of his frightful plans

Alone reposed his head in the tyrant's tent.

I entered. A god led me on, a terrifying idea

Of the death I was bringing—a forewarning dream

Excited his terror in his deep sleep

Presenting him the image of his proscriptions

Some ill-formed sounds of blood and carnage

Escaped his mouth, and his perfidious heart,

Even in rest was deploying its furor

In farcical accents pronouncing "Pompey"

At this name I plunged the sword in his heart.

My rival passed from sleep to death

A too gentle death for so many assassinations

He ought to have perished by an ignominious execution.

I know that of Pompey, it would have been more worthy

To attack a Caesar in the night of battle

But a tyrannous Caesar didn't deserve it.

Silence and death served my retreat.

JULIA

Shivering, I'm experiencing a troubled joy

Terror seized me, corrupting my hope

Secretly poisoned the joy of seeing you.

Can you at least flee from this execrable island?

POMPEY

Me, flee!

JULIA

There remains a formidable tyrant.

POMPEY

If heaven seconds us, he won't stay much longer.

JULIA

And how to calm my lost wits?

Anthony is going to avenge the death of his accomplice.

POMPEY

At this moments the Gods are doing justice to Anthony.

And I shall die, at least, happy in my misfortunes

Over the all bloody bodies of our two oppressors.

Come, there's no longer time to listen to your alarms.

JULIA

Heaven! What are those torches, those screams, that clash of arms?

POMPEY

I no longer see the slave to whom I was entrusted

And who led me among our enemies.

Straight to the bed of Octavian he guided my fury.

(Aufidius and Albina enter)

AUFIDIUS

All will be lost. Fulvia's slave,

Seized by soldiers is already in irons.

The news of Caesar fills the air of the camp.

They are marching, they are in arms;

As to the rest, I'm unaware.

I have soldiers. Let's go.

JULIA (to Aufidius)

Ah! It's you that I implore

It's you who have become Pompey's support.

AUFIDIUS

I can promise you at least to die near him.

POMPEY

Place your courage to endure my ruin.

Fulvia's tent is open at your feet.

Go there, await there the final blows of fate.

Confound your tyrants, still, after my death.

Conserve for all of them an eternal hate.

That's the way to be faithful to Pompey.

For me—living and dying as your spouse.

I will sell them very dearly the life that is yours.

The coward flees in vain; death flies in his entourage.

It's by defying it that the brave avoid it.

CURTAIN

ACT V

Guards at the rear.

JULIA

Indeed, you told me that I needed to fear all.

Look, will you, at the success!

FULVIA

You alone are to be pitied.

You had a bright future before you.

You are losing a fine life, while mine was frightful.

Live—if you dare; I detest life.

My hand didn't suffice to my bold soul.

These monsters that heaven still wants to protect

Are luckier than we in the art of vengeance.

Pompey, when approaching this perfidious Octavian

Thinking to punish him, only struck down a slave.

One of the vile instruments in these bloody conspiracies.

Unworthy of dying at the hand of a hero

Of a great enemy I was going to purge the world.

I marched, I advanced in this profound night

My arm was raised, when on all sides

Relit torches struck my glance

Octavian all bloody appeared in the tent.

An insolent troop of their cowardly lictors

Led me to this place, a captive near you.

Bow to your tyrants, I am bearing their blows here.

Let them let me live, or actually, let them punish me

My vengeance is ruined, and that's my torture.

Heaven! If you still intend to prolong my fate

Let it be only to arm my hands

To better serve my hate and my cheated fury.

JULIA

Alas! Did you learn what has become of Pompey?

Is he living or dead in this bloody desert?

Was Aufidius able to steal this hero

From tyrants so much proscribed that the earth abandons him?

FULVIA

He doesn't dare flatter me with it, but no one suspects

That Pompey is actually wandering about these shores.

Today, near Cesena, all his friends are dead.

The rumor of his death begins to spread.

The tyrants are deceived—and you can understand

That rumors may yet serve to save him.

It's a case that my hands have not been able to reserve to themselves.

You are free at least; his safety concerns you.

You see me captive, I'm arrested, guarded

I can do nothing for you, nor for him, nor for myself.

I'm expecting death.

(Enter Anthony, Octavian, Tribunes.)

ANTHONY

Tribunes, execute my will;

Watch this guilty woman and answer to me for her.

Follow the criminal tracks of her conspiracies

Let her be observed, and especially let us be informed

Of secret accomplices introduced by her.

FULVIA

I have no accomplices and these scornful names

Are for your followers, for your likes

For these new Romans, who, made to serve you,

Dishonor themselves just by obeying you.

Traitor, don't seek the hand that threatens you—

Here it is: you ought to know my audacity

The act of proscription that I learned from you

Instructs me how to ruin you and directs my blows.

I haven't been able to assuage my vengeance on the two of you

I expect it from you alone and your alliance.

I expect it from the crimes that made you friends

They are going to divide you as they united you.

Between parricides there is no friendship.

Jealous of each other, each perfidious to the other,

You both detest each other and the world detests you.

Dragged from ocean to ocean by your faithlessness

One crushed by the other, executioner and victim,

May your numberless ills be equal to your crimes!

Revolted citizens, pretended sovereigns

Who have made a game of human misfortune

Who passing from carnage to the arms of insolence

From murder and from pleasure experience intoxication in peace

My name will become dear to centuries to come

For merely having attempted to punish you.

ANTHONY

Let her be taken away: go.

JULIA (to Octavian)

Ah—suffer that Julia

Accompany Fulvia far from her oppressors

My arm is not armed; only my heart

Is against three of you; my misery, and our laws and gods

You despise them all, but Caesar still

That sacred name for you, that name that Rome honors

Has some authority over your hardened hearts.

Dare you ravish liberty from his blood

Did he think that his fugitive niece

Would become the captive of his adoptive son?

OCTAVIAN

Did he think that Julia, with so much furor

Capable of betraying the honor of the blood that made her?

I don't believe your soul is yet bold enough

To dare share the crimes of Fulvia

But without imputing her senseless crimes to you

The love of Pompey is criminal enough.

JULIA

Yes, I love him, Caesar, and you must believe it.

I love him, I tell you, and I glory in it totally.

I prefer Pompey wandering abandoned

To all powerful Caesar, to Caesar crowned.

Cato, against the gods took the part of his father.

I shall die for the son, his death is more dear to me

Than all the blood of the proscribed is to your eyes

His hand repurchases them; my heart was the prize for it

Don't dispute with him his noble reward.

Caesar, be content with total power.

If he's honored in Rome, and especially in battles

A name of which he's worthy, and which he did not usurp;

If you are jealous of a name that he's revived

Think to equal it, rather than pursue him.

OCTAVIAN

Yes, Caesar is jealous as he is irritated.

I know Pompey's worth, and I am a little flattered by it.

And you—but we are going to deepen the crime.

(Guards, a Tribune enter)

ANTHONY

Well—what have you done?

TRIBUNE

They are bringing the victim.

JULIA

What victim, o heaven!

OCTAVIAN

Who is this wretch?

Where was he found?

TRIBUNE

Near these frightful caverns

In the midst of rocks that were struck by lightning

He reddened the ground with the blood of our soldiers.

Aufidius, a secret confidant of Fulvia,

Died fighting at the side of this traitor.

He barely gave in to numbers, to his wounds

Our cares multiplied in these obscure rocks

Which stopped the torrents of blood he was losing

And recalled life to his bloody members.

It's necessary that he live and in torture,

At least, he will inform you of the names of his accomplices.

ANTHONY

He's one of the proscribed, who, striking at random

Would bring death to us in the parts we share

One ought to have chosen him in a thick crowd.

Casca struck the first blow against Caesar.

I recognize Fulvia and her idle fury

Who will always arm avengers against us.

But I will force her to name this liar.

TRIBUNE

No need; his intrepid rage

Still takes honor in the great attempted murder

He doesn't hide the motive and the author.

OCTAVIAN

You're going pale, Julia.

TRIBUNE

He's coming.

JULIA

Implacable heaven

You are abandoning us!

(Pompey enters, wounded, supported by guards)

OCTAVIAN

Who are you, wretch

Who was able to engage your hand to this unheard of murder?

POMPEY

Is that Octavian who speaks and dares to question me?

TRIBUNE

Respond to the Triumvir!

POMPEY

Well! That funereal name

Well! That frightful title that the world detests

Ought to inform you enough of my duty and my plans.

JULIA

I am dying!

OCTAVIAN

What are they?

POMPEY

Those of all Romans.

ANTHONY

What strange arrogance in a simple soldier,

OCTAVIAN

His firmness astonishes me as much as his valor.

Who exactly are you?

POMPEY

A Roman worthy of a better fate.

OCTAVIAN

What brought you here?

POMPEY

Your punishment, your death.

You know that it is just.

JULIA

At last ours is certain.

POMPEY

I must avenge the insult of the whole world on you.

Learn, Triumvirs, oppressors of mankind,

That it is with Sacevola, as it is with Tarquins.

Even error has deceived me. Lictors who are presenting me

With fire which must punish my too impudent hand

It is ready to fall in the vengeful brazier

Just as it was ready to pierce your heart.

OCTAVIAN

Him, the soldier of Aufidius! At this new outrage,

At this bold speech, and especially at the courage

This Roman deploys before my confounded eyes,

At these features of grandeur spread over his face,

If I were not informed that Pompey in his flight,

At the foot of the Appenines is still braving my pursuit

I would think—but already you are drawing me out of errors

You weep, you tremble—it's Pompey!

JULIA

Ah! lord!

POMPEY

You are not deceived: the Roman who braves you

Who would avenge his country on Anthony and Octavian

Possesses a very fine name, too dear to the world

Not to boast of it in the opprobrium of tatters.

I promised you the head of Pompey in these parts

Strike, masters of the world—it's your conquest.

JULIA

Misfortune!

OCTAVIAN

O fate.

JULIA

O pure blood of heroes!

POMPEY

I haven't been able to equal the labours of my father.

I've given way to these tyrants the way that great man did

And like him, I am dying as the defender of Rome.

JULIA

Octavian, are you satisfied? You hold in your hands

Julia and Pompey, and the fate of mankind.

Do you expect that my cowardly tears will exhaust themselves at your feet?

The weak shed them, tyrants scorn them,

I would reproach myself for the least sigh.

That would be useless, and would cause blushing

I no longer speak to you of the victor of Pharsalia.

If your father wept for his fatal death

He who is nothing but the executioner of Romans

Is not worthy of following so fine an example

Your edicts have proscribed him, tear life from him

But begin with me, start with Julia

So long as I live, your life will be in danger

Go—don't leave me a hero to avenge.

You who dared love me, learn to know me:

Tyrant you are looking at his wife; she's worthy of being so.

OCTAVIAN

By an added crime are they lessening my wrath?

He's only the more guilty by being your spouse

Anthony, you see what our laws demand?

ANTHONY

His death. It's necessary; our legions expect it.

I don't hesitate; Caesar pardoned,

But beneficent Caesar is dead, murdered;

Interests, the times, men—are all different.

I long fought, and I honored his father,

He armed himself nobly for the Roman Senate.

I know his son only as an assassin.

POMPEY

Cowards! You strike your victims with someone else's hands.

I made a virtue of what made your crime.

I was unable to strike you in battle

You had your executioners, I had only my arm.

I save a hundred proscribed and was one myself.

You are it by law; your supreme grandeur

Was your first crime, and deserved death.

By the law of pirates, arbiters of my fate

You think to abase me! You! In your insolence

Know that no mortal will have that power,

Heaven itself, heaven which allows me to perish

Can overwhelm Pompey, but not degrade him.

ANTHONY

You see his fury; it justifies us.

Assure our empire, assure our lives.

JULIA

Barbarians.

OCTAVIAN

I know his wild courage.

And Julia, by loving him, has already condemned him.

ANTHONY

His death was prepared by us for a long while.

It is too legitimate, it is too delayed.

It's you that he attacked, it's you alone who ought

To announce the destiny that you reserve for him.

OCTAVIAN

Then you approve the sentence I am going to render?

ANTHONY

Pronounce it, I'll subscribe to it.

POMPEY

I am ready to hear it

To submit to it.

OCTAVIAN (after a long silence)

I am the master of his fate.

If I were only judge, he would go to death.

I am the son of Caesar, I have his example to follow.

It's up to me to give it. I pardon—he must live.

Anthony, imitate me; I am announcing to the world

That I am finished with murder and proscriptions

They are too harsh. I want Rome to learn—

ANTHONY

So you intend all the hate to fall on me,

Gather up minds to better distance me from them

Seduce Romans—pardon, to reign.

OCTAVIAN

No—I intend to teach you to vanquish vengeance

Love is more terrible, has greater violence;

At my age, perhaps, it ought to carry me away

It battles me still, and I intend to defeat it.

Let's both of us begin a more just rule

Let Octavian be forgotten and let Augustus be cherished.

Be jealous of me, but to better efface

All stains of the blood we had to shed.

Pardon Fulvia, to these remaining wretches,

Proscribed, escaped from our funereal orders

Let us let ourselves be disarmed by human screams

And one day let Rome learn to love us!

(to Julia)

I give you to Pompey by rendering his life

He would have received nothing if he lived without Julia.

(to Pompey)

Be for or against us, defy or submit to our laws

Without fearing you or loving you, I leave you the choice.

Let us support against envy the names of our fathers,

Either generous friends or noble adversaries.

If you believe yourself the avenger of the Roman people

Be my enemy on the field of honor.

Go find a refuge far from the Triumvirate,

I take between the two of us Victory for judge.

Let's not shed any more blood, except in the midst of hazards,

I place myself in the hands of the Gods; they are for the Caesars.

JULIA

Octavian, is this really you? Is it true?

POMPEY

You astonish me.

In vain you have become great; in vain you pardon me.

Rome, the state, the name I bear—make us enemies.

Our fathers have transmitted the hate between us.

It's commanded by them, and like them immortal.

Rome submitting to you calls me to its aid.

I will employ your benefactions but to deliver Rome.

Go—I must save Rome, but I must admire you.

CURTAIN

COMEDY AT FERNEY
BY LOUIS LURINE
AND ALBÉRIC SECOND

Translated and adapted by Frank J. Morlock

CAST OF CHARACTERS

VOLTAIRE

PRINCE DE LIGNE

MONT FERMEIL

JACQUOT

CELIANE

COMEDY AT FERNEY

The action takes place at Voltaire's residence in Ferney in 1765.

A small elegant salon. Center door opens on a garden. On one side French doors open on a park. On the other side a door to Voltaire's rooms. A small hidden door opening to the theatre. Near it, A portrait of the Prince de Ligne. Near the audience Voltaire's desk with a large armchair beside it. A little screen surrounds the desk. A round table and another desk.

Jacquot is alone. He holds a paper in his hand and declaims tragically.

JACQUOT

Vainly you try to separate from me though harshness

Your image is forever graven in my soul.

By Mohammed, believe my Turkish oath

My eternal love is stronger still

Turk! Turk! Turk! Impossible to proceed. Impossible to find a rhyme for Turkish.

(seeing the Prince enter)

Ah, my lord.

(bowing)

PRINCE DE LIGNE (entering and sitting at the round table)

Yes, I will spend fifteen days at Ferney, in the palace of this veritable sovereign that one calls Voltaire. Our dear poet is always in gray slippers, dressed in long stocking up to the knees, large wig, and a little black bonnet. Sunday he puts on a pretty waistcoat with high stockings with buckled shoes and lace right up to his fingers. You ask me forcefully for details. I hope you will be satisfied my dear friend. Goodbye. I will leave tonight or tomorrow, without fail and I will see you in Turin. (he folds up the letter)

Eleven letters since this morning.

(he rings)

JACQUOT (advancing)

Sir?

PRINCE DE LIGNE

Is Voltaire visible?

JACQUOT

My illustrious master prays Your Highness to wait for him here. It seems that the great man is impatient to see you.

PRINCE DE LIGNE

He retired early yesterday: You don't think he could be indisposed?

JACQUOT

No, Milord, we were working, we created some verses.

PRINCE DE LIGNE

What, wiseacre?

JACQUOT

M. de Voltaire has been so gracious as to take me for his private secretary, milord.

PRINCE DE LIGNE

And he consults you as Molière consulted LaForet?

JACQUOT

Better than that, Prince; one day I had the signal honor to propose a rhyme to him and he accepted it.

PRINCE DE LIGNE

Come on—I don't despair to see you ride Pegasus in your turn.

JACQUOT

I am preparing myself in solitary studies.

PRINCE DE LIGNE

Is it an epic poem with which you are disposed to enrich France?

JACQUOT

No, it's a tragedy that I found in the silence of the night.

PRINCE DE LIGNE

A tragedy!

JACQUOT

I've already got my declamation for the third act, my thoughts for the fourth, and my great declamation at the end. Oh, I'm hung up on the rules. Dare I pray Your

Highness to guard my secret?

PRINCE DE LIGNE

Rest easy, Mr. Tragic Author. I swear by the Styx.

JACQUOT

By the Styx. Oath of a great lord, no question. I will remember it.

(aloud)

Here comes the great man.

(Enter Voltaire dressed in his finest attire; he goes to the Prince.)

VOLTAIRE

Good-day, my friend. Have you failed to attend me?

PRINCE DE LIGNE

No, majesty.

VOLTAIRE

Ah, your majesty! You believe in the royalty of a poor poet. You have the goodness to forget your princely title in the home of a hunter of rhymes. As if I always found them. Ask this comedian.

JACQUOT (aside)

The fact is I have one ready for him. If he would only render me the same service.

VOLTAIRE (to Jacquot, showing him a letter)

Tell me, this letter you brought me—this letter this morning. How did it come?

JACQUOT

It came by way of the garden.

VOLTAIRE

In the mail?

JACQUOT

No, sir. In the prettiest little hand I've ever seen.

VOLTAIRE (low)

What—she herself—in person?

(aloud)

My niece didn't see the lady?

JACQUOT

No, sir. Madame Denis had gone out. Today's Sunday;

Madame Denis always listens to masses. One for her, the other for the rest of the house, and I believe she'll spend her whole day at Church.

VOLTAIRE

Good. Go.

(aside)

I'm not angered by her absence.

JACQUOT (low)

Oh—this Turk will take me to the devil.

(Jacquot leaves)

PRINCE DE LIGNE

That leaves me to ask you, my dear Voltaire, if you have need of me this morning?

VOLTAIRE

Oh, I have need of you, of your advice. It's a question of the most serious thing and the most laughable.

PRINCE DE LIGNE

Is it a question of Freron?

VOLTAIRE

Freron's attacks on me are only buffooneries.

PRINCE DE LIGNE

Or is it Frederick the Great?

VOLTAIRE

Don't speak to me of Frederick the Great! I tested this royal philosopher. I found only a vandal. I've sent him back his chamberlain's key, his pensions, his portraits.

PRINCE DE LIGNE

I received them with tenderness, returned them with sighs, as a lover in his just rage tears up the portrait of his mistress.

VOLTAIRE

The King of Prussia! A composition of Caesar and Prussian Caesar!

PRINCE DE LIGNE

Is it a question of Rousseau?

VOLTAIRE

You make me think of that unfortunate. Where is he?

Let him come to me. My arms are open. He's driven from Neufchatel and its environs? Let me find him, lead me to him. All that I possess is his.

PRINCE DE LIGNE (low)

Hum!

(aloud)

Then I see you are going to speak to me of Madame Denis and our great quarrel.

VOLTAIRE

Madame Denis is furious. She believe you're capable of anything.

PRINCE DE LIGNE

It's still a question of your pretty servants? My word, yes! Evenings when they carry fruit and cream, I vainly tried to listen to you and admire you. They distracted me a bit.

VOLTAIRE

I've seen that clearly, O Don Juan. Also, not much later than yesterday, in seeing them walking naked up to their shoulders because of the heat, I took their beautiful necks in both hands, and I exclaimed in anger: Stuffed in like this, stuffed in like that—go to the devil.

PRINCE DE LIGNE

And the devil will thank you for it.

VOLTAIRE

So much the better. If someone needs to have some friends about, it's Voltaire.—Wait, dear prince, I return to my secret.

PRINCE DE LIGNE

A state secret!

VOLTAIRE

A secret of the heart. It's a question of a woman.—Of a woman amorous of a poet, and this poet—it's me. Yes, at my age—who would believe it? It's true, she doesn't know me. This poor woman is crazy. What do you think, my prince?

PRINCE DE LIGNE

The privilege of genius. All the great poets have a cortege of women who adore them,—mysterious creatures, tender, sensitive, credulous—devoted only to passion.

VOLTAIRE

And to ridicule.

PRINCE DE LIGNE

It isn't exactly love. It's devotion—like a god and his priestesses.

VOLTAIRE

The god of Ferney, is old, sick, chagrined—he can do nothing for his devotees. (showing picture)

Ah, if I resembled this picture of yours.

PRINCE DE LIGNE

And how was this great love unveiled to you?

VOLTAIRE

From a distance—in five or six letters. And here's one—the last. The only one which has attracted my attention. Sympathy, perhaps. She speaks to me of my reputation and my glory. She boasts of having devoured my works—in their entirety—one after the other. She recalls my attention to the legend of Tasso and Elenor—what can I tell you? She begs for the precious right of following my feet, to live in the aurora of my glorious house—to serve me, to admire me like the most humble of creatures, thus she says to fly to immortality on the wings of poetry.

PRINCE DE LIGNE

Where is this ambitious adventurer?

VOLTAIRE

I have no idea, but her letter is postmarked Geneva, and announces that my new servant intends a visit this very day.

PRINCE DE LIGNE

What's her name?

VOLTAIRE

Celaine. Celaine Montfermeil.—What do you say about such a love?

PRINCE DE LIGNE

Is this the first good fortune of the type of which you've been the hero?

VOLTAIRE

Assume I've forgotten a little how to behave in these affairs, Don Juan. I need advice. What would you do in my place?

PRINCE DE LIGNE

In your place, Voltaire, I would receive this woman and listen to her—heart to heart. If she's young, if she's pretty, if she's witty, Madame or Miss Celiane perhaps, will charm you, and you will supply her with life. If she's old, ugly or stupid, you will let her die of love and chagrin. She won't have anything better to do.

VOLTAIRE

And if she's worthy to love—what am I to do then?

PRINCE DE LIGNE

Is one disturbed by things like that?

VOLTAIRE

Well—if it disturbs me?

PRINCE DE LIGNE

By an amorous woman who embraces you, as if a memory to pay: one doesn't think about it. The thing happens and there's nothing more to worry about.

VOLTAIRE

Bad faith?

PRINCE DE LIGNE

Practical philosophy. Your little novel is a new book—you can read a few pages of it, if it's amusing, and you can discard it, if it's annoying.

VOLTAIRE

And if the book pleases me so much that I'd like to read it from cover to cover? Also, my vision gets worse every day, my prince.

PRINCE DE LIGNE

Then, my dear Voltaire, one must resort to a reader. In this case, think of me—my vision is still excellent, God be thanked.

JACQUOT (entering)

Sir.

VOLTAIRE

What do you want, Jacquot?

JACQUOT

There's an original—of fifty years of age who asks to speak to you immediately.

VOLTAIRE

His name?

JACQUOT

He refuses to tell me.

VOLTAIRE

What's he .like?

JACQUOT

Like nothing. Passably dressed. I shut the door on him.

VOLTAIRE

You will go bring him back.

(to Prince)

It may be some pleasing personage who wishes to adore the patriarch of Ferney. We will laugh at him if he's going to sing my praises to this small town. Oh, my God, I always think if it were Rousseau.

PRINCE DE LIGNE

I wager this mysterious visitor is simply a tragic actor, a poor devil of a nomad artist, coming to ask you for a letter of recommendation to the Comédie Française.

VOLTAIRE

I am indeed fearful of having an affair—in someway indiscreet that won't amuse us. De Ligne, have a seat—over there—and if I need you to come to our assistance in ridding ourselves of an irritant—(the Prince sits at a distance, and Voltaire sits in his armchair. Jacquot retires after having introduced Montfermeil who comes in stepping softly.)

MONTFERMEIL

This is singular. I'm already uneasy.

PRINCE DE LIGNE (low to Voltaire)

He's worried. The sun dazzles him.

MONTFERMEIL (aside)

Come—a little courage. After all, a great man is only a man.

(advancing)

Which of you gentlemen is named Voltaire?

VOLTAIRE

I am, sir.—You don't recognize me then? You've never seen my portrait?

MONTFERMEIL

Never.

VOLTAIRE (low to Prince)

He's a provincial.

PRINCE DE LIGNE (low)

Say a savage!

MONTFERMEIL

Gentlemen, when I'm tired, I have the bad habit of sitting. I accept this armchair which you haven't offered me.

PRINCE DE LIGNE (low)

Decidedly, he's a Huron.

VOLTAIRE

I hear you.

MONTFERMEIL

When we are alone.

VOLTAIRE

The gentleman is one of my best friends, and one

cannot say anything to him that he cannot hear.

MONTFERMEIL

In fact, in this sort of affair one needs two witnesses. The gentleman will be yours, my cousin will be mine.

VOLTAIRE

Of what sort of affair are you speaking, my dear sir?

MONTFERMEIL

Your dear sir! Mr. Voltaire, one of us is too many to have here. It follows that I am to kill you or be killed by you.

Choose!

PRINCE DE LIGNE (low)

He's mad.

VOLTAIRE

You hate me to such a degree?

MONTFERMEIL

I will kill you. The Muses will carry your casket. It's their right, it's their duty. But I will kill you.

PRINCE DE LIGNE (to Voltaire)

I admire your patience.

VOLTAIRE (to Prince)

Let him speak.

MONTFERMEIL

I am jealous of you, sir.

VOLTAIRE

You write poetry?

MONTFERMEIL

I make watches.

VOLTAIRE

You're a clock-maker?

MONTFERMEIL

From Geneva.

VOLTAIRE

And you made this trip to kill me?

MONTFERMEIL

Immediately. My wife will die of shame—it's possible—but I will be avenged.

VOLTAIRE

Your wife?

MONTFERMEIL

Yes, sir, my wife—for I have a wife—dear to me.

VOLTAIRE

Faith save us, Mr. Clock-maker.

MONTFERMEIL

I deceive myself. She's wife to both of us—and that's what enrages me.

(he sits back down)

PRINCE DE LIGNE (low to Voltaire)

Ah, Voltaire.

VOLTAIRE

On my honor, sir, I don't understand you. If this is a charade, send it to the newspapers.

MONTFERMEIL

You will understand me—I have the misfortune to have a very young, pretty wife.

VOLTAIRE

At the moment it's impossible for me to attend your case.

MONTFERMEIL

By God! If she weren't pretty and young! But—she is poetic, sir, she is sentimental, sir, she makes verses, sir.

VOLTAIRE

Is that any fault of mine?

MONTFERMEIL

Precisely! Your works have turned her head. She is overwhelmed by your wit, your genius, as she puts it! In the day time she is absorbed reading your works—it is impossible for me to snatch a word from her. At night—I have the humiliation to listen to your cursed name spoken with smiling lips as she sleeps. That is why I hate you.

PRINCE DE LIGNE (to Voltaire)

This must be the husband of your admirer.

MONTFERMEIL (facing Voltaire)

I am in business! I need my wife to watch my house, and to care for my papers. (rising)

My wife has established her domicile in seventh heaven—in the stupid country of idle talk, dreams, novels, idle stories. I had chickens, superb chickens, my wife has replaced them with doves—and she talks to them as if the poor creatures were capable of understanding. My garden produced excellent vegetables, now she cultivates nothing but flowers—which are useless—and ruin me.

PRINCE DE LIGNE

But you have such a charming wife there.

MONTFERMEIL

Charming? A mad creature that I always find unexpectedly sad, pensive—her hand on her heart, her eyes turned toward heaven, contemplating the moon. I intend for my wife to contemplate only the face of her husband! (he sits down again)

VOLTAIRE

Your wife is romantic to the point of extravagance. Well—she must be distracted.

MONTFERMEIL

Not later than yesterday I tried to give her a distraction, and offered her diamonds this big. (gesturing) Well, nothing worked. I am not able to give stars for earrings.

VOLTAIRE

You must tire her out. Go about the world, You must secure by dissipation, by pleasure, the poetic shroud which envelops her, and is slowly killing her

MONTFERMEIL

Eh, sir, you forget who I am. Do I have money to run around the world? Have I the time to secure the poetic shroud covering my wife?

VOLTAIRE

I don't know your wife. Your wife doesn't know me. She loves me. She loves me from a distance. A bit further from the shadows. What danger threatens you?

MONTFERMEIL

What dangers! By God, your colleague Mr. Molière didn't trouble himself to call them by their villainous name. The distance which separates Geneva from the shadows of Ferney is quickly traveled. Beside, I know that Celiane has dared to write to you!

PRINCE DE LIGNE (low)

I was right.

VOLTAIRE

Celiane, you say?

MONTFERMEIL

Don't deny it. I am certain.

VOLTAIRE (rising quickly)

Can I descend to a lie, me, a gentleman?

Yes, I've received a letter from your wife. The sixth.

MONTFERMEIL (also rising)

Misfortune!

VOLTAIRE

I am expecting here here in an hour.

MONTFERMEIL

All right. Then I am going to kill you both.

VOLTAIRE

Listen to me, my dear chap! You are the extreme limit

of the absurd.

MONTFERMEIL

Sir—

VOLTAIRE

Don't cross her.

PRINCE DE LIGNE (aside)

It's done.

MONTFERMEIL

But, sir—

VOLTAIRE

I've been patient. Have some patience in your turn.

MONTFERMEIL

What do you want me to do?

MONTFERMEIL

Greet your wife.

MONTFERMEIL

Alone.

VOLTAIRE

Alone.

MONTFERMEIL

A tête-à-tête?

VOLTAIRE

Exactly.

MONTFERMEIL

And I?

VOLTAIRE

In the meanwhile, you will explore my park—it's worth the trouble.

MONTFERMEIL

Do you take me for a clown?

VOLTAIRE

You know some literature, I see that. So much the better. Do you know the apology of the floating sticks?

MONTFERMEIL

In the distance it's something.

VOLTAIRE

And nearby it's nothing. This is the same. Your wife has no question created a great man—in her fantasy—still young, gallant, superb. I will show her the Voltaire of reality. A poor man who for several years hasn't had any kisses except the playful ones of his niece, Madame Denis.

MONTFERMEIL (low)

In fact—all Voltaire as he is. Most are better preserved.

(aloud)

You will do this?

VOLTAIRE

Ah—didn't I tell you that I've done it these ten years?

MONTFERMEIL

And you will give me back my wife?

VOLTAIRE

Yes.

MONTFERMEIL

Cured?

VOLTAIRE

I hope so.

MONTFERMEIL

Soon?

VOLTAIRE

Soon as I can.

MONTFERMEIL

Then I won't be separated?

VOLTAIRE

It's convenient.

MONTFERMEIL

Can't you hide me in a nearby room where I will be able to listen?

VOLTAIRE

Go to the park or I won't answer for anything.

MONTFERMEIL

Wait—

VOLTAIRE

My last word.

MONTFERMEIL

I obey.

PRINCE DE LIGNE (aside)

I promise to witness this myself.

MONTFERMEIL (aside)

I'll try to observe them.

VOLTAIRE

Go this way. You won't meet your wife.

MONTFERMEIL

Exactly! Decidedly a great man is a bit more than a man.

(he leaves)

PRINCE DE LIGNE (rising)

Well played—oh my illustrious friend—and this poor man goes off reassured.

VOLTAIRE

Isn't he correct to do so?

PRINCE DE LIGNE

This worthy Montfermeil—who for two hours will consciously advise the young saplings of your park and your garden! It's comedy, Voltaire.

VOLTAIRE

I spoke seriously, I swear it.

PRINCE DE LIGNE

To others, dear friend, to others.

VOLTAIRE

I swear to you, de Ligne, that I won't fall short in any respect of keeping the promises I've made to this honest married man.

PRINCE DE LIGNE

Truly?

VOLTAIRE

Truly..

JACQUOT (entering)

Sir, the lady of the letter is here—she's waiting.

(the Prince looks out the window)

VOLTAIRE

Let her come in.

(Jacquot exits.)

VOLTAIRE (aside)

Yes, at least there's time for me to dream up some ingenious way—

(aloud)

De Ligne, what trick, what comedy could I well invent?

PRINCE DE LIGNE

You ask me, me—you, Voltaire?

(he turns back to the window)

VOLTAIRE

My oath! I will do like the great actors. I will wait for the footlights, the public, and the inspiration. Come, come, dear prince—the curtain rises and I'm not yet in costume.

(Votaire exits.)

PRINCE DE LIGNE (alone, still looking out the window)

Ah, Voltaire, seeing the patient, I scorn the medicine. This young woman is totally charming. I will dream of her,

(He exits by the hidden door. After a moment, Jacquot and Celiane enter)

JACQUOT

Enter, Madame.

CELIANE

Voltaire really intends to see me, you say?

JACQUOT

The great man is waiting for you, madame.

CELIANE

This salon is his—this is where he works.

JACQUOT

Yes, madame it is where we cultivate The Graces and The Muses. It's right here, with this pen that we wrote Tancred and The Orphan of China.

CELIANE

I feel transported by joy and my own audacity.

JACQUOT

Have the goodness to wait, Madame. I am going to inform the great man.

(aside)

By Mohammed—believe my Turkish oath—and still it won't rhyme.

(he leaves)

CELIANE

I am in Voltaire's home. I will hear him. Not just seeing or listening to him alone, drunken with looking at him, with his word, with his genius. I tremble with surprise, pride and joy. I believe in listening to charming persons, all the heroes of my past who speak to me of glory—almost divine of their father. Yes, I astonish myself to listen to some confused voices telling me about all the admirable creations of an enchanter named Voltaire.—I am quite proud and indeed, happy. I would make him wait. I would have hours—days—to look at each piece of furniture, each picture, each book—every separate object in this room that the hand of the great man touches.

(seeing a portrait of the Prince de Ligne)

That's him, without a doubt. Yes, it is his precise image, I am sure of it. If I dared—if it were possible for a profane creature to imagine bad verse in the house of poetry. O my poor wit—you don't value my heart. Oh, if the heart could write! But no—it must think—seek work to write—and I only know how to dream. Is the heart then not witty?

(taking a pen)

The pen of Voltaire in the hand of a woman, it's as though I were holding the world.

JACQUOT (entering)

Monsieur de Voltaire.

(he leaves)

CELIANE (throwing the pen onto the table and collapsing into an armchair)

Heavens!

VOLTAIRE (looking at her)

Not too bad, it seems to me—for a little bourgeoise—married to a pedantic fellow.

CELIANE (aside)

I cannot see or hear any more.

VOLTAIRE (aside)

Come—she's seen me in heaven—now she'll see me on earth.

CELIANE (aside)

Dare I look at him?

VOLTAIRE

Eyes lowered, hands joined—like a devotee praying to a god she cannot see.

—Is it you then, Madame, who take the trouble to address me with several exclamation points? In reading your last letter which announced to me your visit—from admiration I've failed to take a little Tronchin: that means, Madame. That I've thought of making myself ill for a day to escape the incense of your gracious homage.

CELIANE (without looking)

Alas—perhaps I'd better return tomorrow.

VOLTAIRE

In time. (aside) The husband will be satisfied with me. I am going to speak marvels.

(aloud)

You are from Geneva. What do you say of Geneva?

CELIANE

It's my country.

VOLTAIRE

You've got a frightful country there.

CELIANE

The nation is cherished by all hearts born there.

VOLTAIRE

Oh—that's only a verse—a verse from Tancred I believe. But it's not true. Aren't you of French descent?

CELIANE

Yes—and daughter of Madame Fontaine-Montel, who

inspired your so beautiful verse.

VOLTAIRE

Madame Fontaine-Montel...it's possible. I made so many verses for so many ladies—not counting the Graces and the Muses. Eh, my God! I will even make one for you if you please to ask for it.

CELIANE

For me? Today?

VOLTAIRE

Instantly. A good poet is a quick worker, always prepared, tireless—if necessary. Isn't your name Celiane? (leaning his elbows on her armchair)

Here, Madame, for you

(aside) All purpose verse.

(aloud)

To Celiane—

If you want me to love again

Make me young again

In the twilight of my life

Join if you can the dawn

From the beautiful glade where the god of wine

With Cupid holds sway.

Time, which leads me by the hand

Warns me to retire.

From its infallible rigor

Let's gain some advantage.

He who lacks the spirit of his age

Gets great misfortune from his age.

CELIANE

What honor! What joy! I will be immortal!

VOLTAIRE

Yes—immortality is a fine thing in the Christian religion—

CELIANE

And in history?

VOLTAIRE

History is a little noise one makes around tombs.

(sitting near her)

Between ourselves, Madame, does the nose of the living revive the dead? But, I am wandering—you came to visit a poet, and you haven't looked at him yet. Raise your eyes to me—deign to look at what you profess to admire.—What you love, madame—and judge.

(Celiane slowly turns and represses a scream as she rises.)

CELIANE

Heavens, you deceive me—it's not Voltaire.

VOLTAIRE

Of whom are you speaking, Madame? Of the poet you dreamed about or the man who woke you up? The poet is still buried alive amidst his poems. The man is before you, and you see—he's made of prose like everybody else.

CELIANE (aside)

Is it possible I am mad?

MONTFERMEIL (opening the door at the right)

Oh—the fine man. He's made himself even uglier than I am. My wife will return to me.

(He retires, but Voltaire has seen him.)

VOLTAIRE

Come, a portrait of Voltaire in the manner of that scamp, Freron.

(aloud)

You think, doubtless, to find here at Voltaire's home a demi-god covered with a singular glow, with laurels on his head, and a harp in his hand? Alas, pretty lady, when one meets me, when one looks at me, when one wishes to see the way I live, I become again a simple mortal—a rich man—almost a gentleman—a Count of Ferney—by right of proprietorship. I work from vocation and pride, I economize my small fortune which is very great. I throw incense to God, and I build a church. I flatter the nobility that I hate, and the people whom I disdain. I criticize the entire world—nothing more witty than my critiques. I am a great philosopher—because I excel at deluding life with songs and stories. I don't have to be approved of, because I astonish. If they fear me, I find I am better loved. I upset posterity by laughing. I seek out public opinion to baffle it. I mock both my enemies and my friends; I think of my admirers to render them ridiculous. I speak willingly to my colleagues to slander them if they are worth an ingenious slander. And for my protectors I have only epigrams. I play an eternal comedy for the meager pleasures of Europe here at Ferney between the screens.

(rising)

I caper on my century as if on dry straw that only awaits fire from heaven. Now, Madame, I believe in nothing less than universal abyss or wind which pushes ever onward. I love nothing, not even creative love, they say, after God.

(low)

O Nonotte, O Patouillet! If you heard Voltaire now.

CELIANE

And Glory, sir, Glory?

VOLTAIRE

Oh, glory is a hypocrite that covers us with flowers, the better to strangle us 1 It will kill me with roses. When I appear in the world, glory accompanies me, glory flatters me, glory caresses me, glory applauds me. Glory creates a theatrical spectacle for me of public credulity. Then it leads me to my doorway. I kiss her from politeness. I say to her: G'night, my love. Then she goes to bed.

I fill my nose with Spanish snuff, and sleep in my turn, cursing Freron.

(taking snuff)

CELIANE (rising)

Is this my worthy poet? My God, where have all the beautiful things gone that once ravished me as if they had come from heaven?

(falling back in her armchair)

VOLTAIRE

Child, you will find all these pretty things—in your library! Admire great men—don't fall in love with them. Poets guard for themselves alone the riches of wit, and the treasures of the imagination, they are misers of their divine fortune, and—under pretext of leaving a rich heritage to posterity—for them, sentiment, inspiration, enthusiasm, genius—all this is simply a magnificent lie, a type of false gold which they sprinkle through the pages of literature.—Wait. Listen to the birds singing in my park. These are the true poets.— Well—do you still wish to become the miserable servant of a celebrated writer. You will be adored in verse for a week, mistrusted after that—in prose, disgusted a little bit later—and unhappy the remainder of your life, But, in your turn, you will perhaps be immortal.

PRINCE DE LIGNE (opening the hidden door)

Ah, Voltaire—how you treat poetry.

(He retires, Celiane drops a tear)

VOLTAIRE

(aside, watching the door)

Decidedly, I have an audience!

(aloud)

What—you are crying, Madame?

CELIANE

Voltaire never cries.

VOLTAIRE

Pardon—I sometimes cry. With one eye, when I need to make others cry.

CELIANE (rising)

Goodbye, I am going to find my poet.

VOLTAIRE

In my main works, you are right.

(taking her hand)

You are wearing a magnificent jewel—do you think it the work of a god or a fairy? No—it was manufactured in a hovel by a vulgar artisan who knew his work.

(kissing her hand)

From now on, you are my friend. Accept for today, the hospitality that I offer you! You will dine with us, and this evening, at the hour which you choose for your departure.

CELIANE

You forget that I left an honest man this morning—who is no doubt waiting for me.

VOLTAIRE

That's right. Don't forget your husband. And I myself will be enchanted to know him. Deign to sit at this table: take this pen and paper and write to your husband. I dictate.

CELIANE (aside)

What am I going to say to my husband under Voltaire's

dictation?

(sitting down)

VOLTAIRE (dictating)

My husband, you know my admiration for the celebrated author of Merope, The Henriade, and Candide. I wanted to see this universal genius. Ah, the cruel disappointment of a woman's enthusiasm. What floating sticks are all these great men—

(interrupting)

What did you say, Madame?

CELIANE

Continue—

VOLTAIRE

I see that you are of my opinion. I continue.

(dictating)

Voltaire is simply a mortal who sits as lord of the village. I was looking for a demi-god, and I found only a good man! Here I am on the Olympus of Ferney until this evening. They insist that I wait for you and I will do so. My friend, the stars in the tunic of my Apollo very much resemble a basin coat. See you soon. And don't be jealous of my dreams.

CELIANE

My husband will thank you, sir

MONTFERMEIL (opening the door at the right)

Oh, yes—her husband thanks you. Now I can go view your grand park—oh great man!

(retiring)

VOLTAIRE (aside)

Let's not lose sight of the Prince de Ligne—quickly this letter to Montfermeil.

(aloud)

I ask your permission to retire, Madame search, dig, in this scribbling, in these books, and you will still find poetry—without the poet! Ah, ah—poets! Those rascals make me think of what the Duke de Nevers said when he saw a supberb herd of sheep pass by. "Perhaps, in all those sheep, there's not a single one that is tender."

(He kisses Celiane's hand and leaves.)

CELIANE (alone)

Am I dreaming? What blasphemies against God, against humanity, against poetry! This poet who provides the world with illusions hasn't even the illusion of his own genius or his own glory. Voltaire only wants to be a drone in poetry and prose. He is doing a job—a function. Ah! my husband was right. A great man is not forced to be handsome, elegant or distinguished.

(examining the portrait of the Prince de Ligne)

And I who expected him to appear with the features of this brilliant gentleman.

JACQUOT (enters with a sack of money)

He's a great man, isn't he Madame?

(depositing the sack on the desk)

Here's what rejoices him—money sent from our publisher in Paris,. The scoundrel was late a week, and we had to give our attorney the order to pursue him.

CELIANE

For being a week late?

JACQUOT

Eh, Madame, do you believe we live on poetry and coffee?

CELIANE

Like master, like valet!

(aloud)

Then there are these great poets who dupe the entire world in creating their masterpieces. When they write, addressing the echoes of the crowd, they ask only for renown, for glory—When they address their own conscience they think only of ambition and money.

JACQUOT

You speak quite at your ease, Madame. Who doesn't need money—much money to do all sorts of great things?

CELIANE

Yes, to increase a small fortune which is already large enough—to become a gentleman by right of property—to play lord of the village—is it possible?

JACQUOT

No, Madame—to give bread to the poor—to aid the

needy.

CELIANE

Then Voltaire is charitable?

JACQUOT

But for Madame Denis, who holds the purse strings we'd be finished off by the demands of charity. And our workers—we have them everywhere. We manufacture watches as much as Geneva. We make work for the poor people who love us.

CELIANE

They say your master disdains the poor people that love you.

JACQUOT

Bah! That's noise bad folk make to cause us to fight with the good. And the poetasters, and the shabby little writers that we protect. We gave a dowry to Miss Corneille.

CELIANE

Is that true? Why, then your master is a sort of Providence.

JACQUOT

He's a demi-god, Madame

(picking up his sack)

She didn't know us, and now she does.

CELIANE

Sir, you are around him, listen to him all the time—is it true that he scorns his genius and his glory?

JACQUOT

Let God be pleased to give us a little less glory and a bit more peace!

Madame Denis who doesn't make verse is right to tell us in the morning, "Oh, God, glory, always glory, What do you do with so much glory?"

CELIANE (aside)

Perhaps he deceived me—but that's all right, I thank him.

(sits absorbed in a reverie. The Prince enters and gestures for Jacquot to shut up and leave—which he does.)

PRINCE DE LIGNE (aside)

That fool came to my aid without knowing it. Voltaire has gone very far. My great friend played an improvised scene. He's not the only doctor to speak ill of himself—in the interest of his patient.

(Going to Celiane and smiling, saluting her)

CELIANE (rising)

Ah—who are you, sir? What do you want?

PRINCE DE LIGNE

Who am I? Look at me, Madame, do you think I flatter myself much on my handsome looks?

(indicating his portrait as he leads her across the room)

Without a doubt, you are disgusted by poetry. I've committed a great sin and I repent. For the honor of poets, Madame, I am coming to repair my stupidity and ask for your pardon.

CELIANE

Your pardon?

PRINCE DE LIGNE

I see that I must absolutely oblige you to know me.

CELIANE

How can I know you—an unknown?

PRINCE DE LIGNE

Have you read the stories of Mr. Boufflers?

CELIANE

What singular story are you telling me, sir?

PRINCE DE LIGNE

It's an ingenious recital—a little history called the Woman and the Physician.

CELIANE

I don't remember it.

PRINCE DE LIGNE

Permit me to remind you of it. There was once a ravishing lady who heard of the genius of a brilliant poet, celebrated and acclaimed—near her. So often and so well—that she decided to love him. Fatigued by adoring him from a distance, she resolved to go to see him. She wrote to this magician as if he was the devil himself and he consented to see her.

CELIANE

I remember now.

PRINCE DE LIGNE

Oh, how she trembles, Madame—from joy or fear in touching the door way of the house of poetry, Then the voice of the poet made itself heard. This young woman listened in silence, eyes lowered—suddenly raised her head and uttered a cry of surprise—a cry of sorrow—in recognizing—actually, no—she recognized nobody, Madame—all this wit, all this grace, this genius which had enchanted her—in books.

CELIANE

Yes—yes—I know all that was only an illusion, a pretty dream. "Oh," said the poor madwoman, shedding a tear. "it's the same with poets as with oracles—one must hear them and adore them—from a distance."

PRINCE DE LIGNE

Some minutes before the happy apparition of Celiane, the poet had received some advice from some bad advisers. He promised them to play doctor for a day—in the interest of a pretty, sick lady. And he tried to achieve this charitable promise by saying—by slandering, by disfiguring—by an audacious comic character.

CELIANE

A comic character?

PRINCE DE LIGNE

Sad comedy, very well played, by a true comedian, an actor of the Théâtre Française stopping by at Ferney.—You are quite back to your mad enthusiasm—there's no danger to fear. A relapse is impossible. Allow me then, Madame, to reoccupy my place, and to present the poet to you.

CELIANE

You, sir—a poet? Voltaire?

PRINCE DE LIGNE

God be praised, Voltaire renounces to science and society the frightful role of doctor. He kneels at your feet. He thanks you. He admires you in his turn—he writes with his eyes fixed on yours:

I adore you, charming Egeria

Why have you inflamed me so late

Why have I wasted the good days of my life

They are lost—And I've never loved.

(aside)

Unpublished verses by Voltaire.

CELIANE

Speak, speak—bid the doctor be gone and the poet to return at once.

PRINCE DE LIGNE

This very day, in this room, I reread your last letter. In that moment, I tried to picture you, and I believed I had already had the honor of seeing you. I contemplated you from a distance, in a world that was the creation of my thoughts, my desires; I closed my eyes and you appeared to my mind as a divine statue of inspiration! Kissing each word of your letter, I said to myself—the heart has its vocation, just as the mind does; my vocation condemns me to be amorous of Celiane—I suffer, but I will love her, and love which suffers finds a secret delight in suffering.

CELIANE

He is there—he's speaking to me; I'm no longer dreaming—happiness awakens me!

PRINCE DE LIGNE

Well, Madame, I was there in my adoration, in my ecstasy, when a poor devil appeared to me, and said:

"My wife is so silly as to adore you—save my wife." This honest man who supplicated me with prayerful hands—is called, I believe, Montfermeil.

CELIANE

My husband!

(aside)

My husband with Voltaire—to laugh at me, to make me ridiculous!

PRINCE DE LIGNE

It was your husband, madam, and, in both your interests, I intended that no one should impersonate me. I permitted a facile scamp to curse the poetry in my name—to profane the glory, to outrage posterity, to deny the God of this world—and the loves which were created in his image.

CELIANE

My God, my God!

PRINCE DE LIGNE

And there's no point in it—enough lies and blasphemy. I am intervening in this comedy—the saddest, the most sordid character—money! Voltaire corresponding with solicitors. In truth—I had too much imagination this morning! Don't believe my enemies, madam—Voltaire lives in beautiful verse and good deeds—his best poem, perhaps, is his own life.

CELIANE (aside)

Ah—each of these words cures a wound in my heart.

PRINCE DE LIGNE

Pardon me, madam, for reclaiming from pride, perhaps, the character and spirit of a poet you once loved without seeing—but that seeing today, you now hate.

CELIANE

Hate you? How could I hate the poetry I've loved so much?

(giving her hand to the Prince)

PRINCE DE LIGNE (aside)

Decidedly she adores poetry.

(aloud)

No—kisses from tender lovers

No—these moments are worth a thousand caresses

Moments so soft and cloying

They're not worth one look from your eyes.

(aside, looking out the window)

The husband!

(taking her arm and moving her away)

CELIANE

Why do you always call me Egeria in your lovely verses?

PRINCE DE LIGNE

Why?—Because henceforth you are my advisor, my angel of inspiration—the familiar genius of this poet.

I had not lived till the day your soul

Penetrated me with its divine heat

On that day—delivered to you

The world disappeared for me.

(The Prince hurries Celaine out—Montfermeil enters from another direction.)

MONTFERMEIL

Ah, Voltaire's right—his park is a beautiful park. But

where is he? I am in a hurry to express my thanks. And to think that this morning I wanted to kill him. Guilty thought! Such an illustrious poet—who dresses so grotesquely. I am going to buy his portrait. I want my wife to have the image of her hero—in a gray cap and glasses. Poor Celiane, by now she must be awfully ashamed. Reassure yourself, my sweet—I will spare you the least reproach—you are punished enough this way. But where is she? Is she hiding her disenchantment and confusion?

(Seeing Jacquot enter)

Sir, hey, sir. You haven't seen my wife.

JACQUOT

Ah—that young lady—the letter lady—is your wife? As to letters: this one for you.

MONTFERMEIL (aside)

My wife's letter—dictated by Voltaire. Mighty fine.

(putting the letter in his pocket, aloud)

Where is she—do you know?

JACQUOT

In the great man's company, I suppose.

MONTFERMEIL

I have the most intense desire that she be unaware of my presence at Ferney. Can I count on you?

(slipping his purse to Jacquot)

Being discreet?

JACQUOT

Dare, sir, dare.

MONTFERMEIL

You promise me secrecy?

JACQUOT

I swear it to you—by the Styx.

MONTFERMEIL (low)

By the Styx. A poetic oath. The favorite oath of Voltaire. I'll remember that.

JACQUOT

Here's the patriarch.

(aside)

Always the Turk.

(Jacquot leaves as Voltaire enters from a different direction)

VOLTAIRE

I am furious! These nobles do whatever they please.

MONTFERMEIL

How agitated he is!

VOLTAIRE (turning toward Montfermeil)

Ah, my dear sir, you are the Prince de Ligne—but you forget I am Voltaire and that name obliges! In my own house!

What audacity! I will write a page in wrath against the nobility and send it to the Duke de Richelieu.

(sits down)

MONTFERMEIL (aside)

He's composing a tragedy.

VOLTAIRE

What are you doing here? Run after your wife.

MONTFERMEIL

My wife? Oh, I'm very easy now. Ah, sir—there alone with me—do you know what I know?

VOLTAIRE

You upset my clock.

MONTFERMEIL

I sing your praises—hidden here.

VOLTAIRE

You saw and heard—I know it.

MONTFERMEIL

You know everything. You are a sorcerer.

VOLTAIRE

I know some things which you don't.

MONTFERMEIL

I don't doubt that, universal man. Oh Mr. Voltaire, you cannot imagine how ugly you look in that get-up.

VOLTAIRE (getting up)

What the devil, sir!

MONTFERMEIL

And I was so unfortunate as to be jealous of you! Why, you look like Celiane's grandfather.

VOLTAIRE

Do you believe, anyone would take you for her husband?

MONTFERMEIL

As you have demonstrated that she would be a madwoman to fall in love with a poet. The true poets are the birds—you said it yourself.—I will buy her a blackbird.— Ah, sir—all my blood is yours.

VOLTAIRE

Eh! What would you have had me do?

MONTFERMEIL

You promised to cure my wife and she' cured.

VOLTAIRE (aside)

The fool. She's never been so sick

MONTFERMEIL

You say?

VOLTAIRE

What's this you're telling me? I've already told you to join your wife. She's waiting impatiently for you.

MONTFERMEIL

Right. I've received the letter of invitation. It's time I appeared.

VOLTAIRE

It's always time for a husband to appear.

MONTFERMEIL

But where is she?

VOLTAIRE

In the garden in the park. Go, go—my poor friend.

MONTFERMEIL

How sadly you say that?

VOLTAIRE

I say it as I feel it. My park is full of traps—a misfortune might happen suddenly.

MONTFERMEIL

Traps!—I'm on my way.

(he goes out hurriedly)

VOLTAIRE (watching him go)

In the alley of sighs—no question she's there.

(Celiane enters)

(aside)

There she is.

CELIANE (not seeing Voltaire)

Voltaire didn't forbid me to follow him to his room. He loves me—he says he will always love me Oh, beautiful promises in verse and in prose. A poet who talks like that is a dangerous book for a woman.

(seeing Voltaire, aside)

I recognize him without his costume. It's the actor.

(aloud)

I congratulate you, sir, you played your role well.

VOLTAIRE

You're indulgent, madam.

CELIANE

I am just. Oh—you are a very convincing actor.

VOLTAIRE

Don't flatter me—I've found my master.

CELIANE

Is it possible?

VOLTAIRE

It's true.

CELIANE

Where?

VOLTAIRE

Right here.

CELIANE

At Ferney?

VOLTAIRE

Precisely.

CELIANE

There are other actors at Ferney?

VOLTAIRE

It would appear so. The rival of whom I speak is a comedian of the best and worst species. He imposes on his audience, dominates it, fascinates it—a predatory artist.

CELIANE

His name?

VOLTAIRE (continuing)

I can judge him without passion. We don't work for the same employer.

VOLTAIRE

Is he young?

VOLTAIRE

Yes, madam, he is young. As for me, I am old. My age condemns me to the role of noble fathers, confidants.

I play them well—not being able to act badly. I appear at the denouement to punish vice and reward virtue. I protect the weakness of women and try to defend the honor of husbands.

CELIANE

That's a fine role, sir.

VOLTAIRE

Say a sacrificial role, madam—of great utility, the more useless. As for the other, the young knight, the Marquis, the Moncade—he dares all—he mocks all—he plays with love.

CELIANE

A difficult character!

VOLTAIRE

Eh, madame, the devil has given him everything—wit, beauty, audacity—a fine memory. He talks of nothing except a heart. Oh, this great comedian—who never appears in the theatre of any country. He does his work traveling. He plays his eternal comedy just as in a palace for a Queen as in a salon of a little bourgeoise.

CELIANE

And—has he played some play of Voltaire's?

VOLTAIRE

Madam, he played The Impertinent. He played another, a real comedy this time. He has betrayed Voltaire's confidence—he has taken his name, he has stolen Voltaire's charming verses—and he has maimed them, the scoundrel—the wretch!

CELIANE (aside)

What's he talking about?

VOLTAIRE

And under the pretext of rehabilitating poetry in the imagination of a woman, he has slandered a poet, his host, and his friend. Oh, my niece is right. That man is capable of anything.

CELIANE

Your niece?

VOLTAIRE

Eh, yes, Madame Denis. But you are in my home and I won't permit it. It goes to my honor and my spirit! My house is like glass—everyone watches me.

I intend that they see me doing the right thing—or at least trying to do it. When one passes for a man of genius, one must at least be an honest man.

CELIANE

It was Voltaire!

MONTFERMEIL (entering)

Ah—there's my wife.

VOLTAIRE

Come, dear Prince, I'm speaking of you. I'm praising you.

PRINCE DE LIGNE (aside, entering)

I don't believe it

MONTFERMEIL

A prince?

CELIANE (looking at Voltaire)

He is indeed Voltaire!

VOLTAIRE (presenting the Prince to Celiane)

The Prince de Ligne.

CELIANE

As, my lord.

PRINCE DE LIGNE (low to Celiane)

What's wrong? I was doing my best to aid poetry and poets.

MONTFERMEIL

Sweetheart, I received your letter and I find it admirable. There's points of wit in this little letter that do great honor to Mr. Voltaire. How you mistreat poets. Now, you know them.

CELIANE (looking at it)

And I haven't ceased to admire them—to esteem them.

MONTFERMEIL (aside)

That's mere politeness.

PRINCE DE LIGNE

Monsieur de Montfermeil, This morning I conceived a vast esteem for your person and your character—think of that.

MONTFERMEIL

Oh, my prince. Without being suited to a T.

PRINCE DE LIGNE

Think of that, I tell you. I am leaving this evening. I offer you a place in my carriage.

MONTFERMEIL

So much honor.

(aside)

He overloads me.

PRINCE DE LIGNE

You appear to regret that the state of your fortune doesn't permit you to give Madame sufficient distractions—such as travel. I am going to Turin. Would you like to accompany me?

MONTFERMEIL

Both of us?

PRINCE DE LIGNE

Both of you!

MONTFERMEIL

Me—visit Italy.

(aside)

He overwhelms me—this guy.

CELIANE

Enough, my dear. We cannot travel—except that I may absent myself sometimes to thank Mr. Voltaire—

(to Voltaire)

If you will permit me.

VOLTAIRE (low, going to Celiane)

Mighty fine.

(to Montfermeil)

I hope, sir, that you will not be jealous of me.

MONTFERMEIL

I swear it.

(aside)

Flatter him a bit.

(aloud)

I swear it by the Styx.

VOLTAIRE

By the Styx. Singular oath for a clock-maker.

PRINCE DE LIGNE (low to Voltaire)

I am sure you have been pitiless with me.

VOLTAIRE

You were without pity for her. What did you say to this poor Celiane, while walking in the park?

PRINCE DE LIGNE

All I did was recite a little poem.

VOLTAIRE

In free verse?

PRINCE DE LIGNE

On my oath—'twas yours.

VOLTAIRE

You did well. At least you have taste. Come! I saw each of you play your role—and we have had a Comedy at Ferney.

CURTAIN

ABOUT THE EDITOR

Frank J. Morlock has written and translated many plays since retiring from the legal profession in 1992. His translations have also appeared on Project Gutenberg, the Alexandre Dumas Père web page, Literature in the Age of Napoléon, Infinite Artistries.com, and Munsey's (formerly Blackmask). In 2006 he received an award from the North American Jules Verne Society for his translations of Verne's plays. He lives and works in México.

www.ingramcontent.com/pod-product-compliance
Lightning Source LLC
LaVergne TN
LVHW041618070426
835507LV00008B/315